USING FRACTIONS

AGS

by
Fulta M. Hilliard

AGS®

American Guidance Service, Inc.
4201 Woodland Road
Circle Pines, MN 55014-1796
1-800-328-2560

Life Skills Mathematics

Printed in the United States of America

ISBN 0–7854–0956–4 (Previously ISBN 0–88671–724–8)

Product Number 90864

A 0 9 8 7 6

Contents

A Work each problem carefully and write your answer in the space provided.

Example:

```
    5
  + 3
    8
```

1.
```
    9
    6
  + 4
```

2.
```
    1
  + 9
```

3.
```
    0
  + 7
```

4.
```
    8
    4
    8
    3
  + 8
```

5.
```
   64
   32
   93
  + 70
```

6.
```
    9
  − 5
```

7.
```
   64
  − 61
```

8.
```
    8
  − 6
```

9.
```
  775
 − 261
```

10.
```
  102
  − 80
```

11.
```
    0
  x 2
```

12.
```
    1
  x 3
```

13.
```
   47
  x 5
```

14.
```
   83
  x 7
```

15.
```
   79
  x 4
```

16. 3)15

17. 4)28

18. 7)56

19. 9)81

20. 5)25

21.
```
  476
  x 9
```

22.
```
  692
 − 540
```

23.
```
  $8.25
   4.16
   9.04
 + .45
```

24. 6)13

25.
```
  596
 − 467
```

26.
```
  $47.96
 − 3.11
```

27.
```
  117
  x 12
```

28. 7)241

29.
```
  791
 + 823
```

30.
```
  $9.17
   3.09
  10.34
 + .62
```

Test Yourself

B Work each problem carefully and write your answer in the space provided.

1.
$$\begin{array}{r} 62 \\ -42 \\ \hline \end{array}$$

2.
$$\begin{array}{r} 0 \\ +8 \\ \hline \end{array}$$

3.
$$\begin{array}{r} 863 \\ -572 \\ \hline \end{array}$$

4.
$$\begin{array}{r} 653 \\ \times\ 9 \\ \hline \end{array}$$

5. $7\overline{)25}$

6.
$$\begin{array}{r} \$14.76 \\ 52.34 \\ 18.00 \\ 7.90 \\ +72.63 \\ \hline \end{array}$$

7.
$$\begin{array}{r} 6,382 \\ \times\ \ 6 \\ \hline \end{array}$$

8. $9\overline{)197}$

9.
$$\begin{array}{r} \$9.61 \\ -1.38 \\ \hline \end{array}$$

10.
$$\begin{array}{r} 8 \\ -0 \\ \hline \end{array}$$

11.
$$\begin{array}{r} 97 \\ \times 87 \\ \hline \end{array}$$

12. $8\overline{)513}$

13. $23\overline{)978}$

14.
$$\begin{array}{r} \$8.05 \\ -6.90 \\ \hline \end{array}$$

15.
$$\begin{array}{r} 205 \\ \times 18 \\ \hline \end{array}$$

16. $31\overline{)756}$

17.
$$\begin{array}{r} 540 \\ \times 83 \\ \hline \end{array}$$

18.
$$\begin{array}{r} \$8.32 \\ 7.19 \\ 9.04 \\ .44 \\ \hline \end{array}$$

19.
$$\begin{array}{r} \$6.10 \\ -4.75 \\ \hline \end{array}$$

20.
$$\begin{array}{r} \$3.00 \\ -1.28 \\ \hline \end{array}$$

21.
$$\begin{array}{r} 34 \\ \times 36 \\ \hline \end{array}$$

22.
$$\begin{array}{r} \$813.50 \\ -29.43 \\ \hline \end{array}$$

23.
$$\begin{array}{r} 254 \\ \times 18 \\ \hline \end{array}$$

24. $8\overline{)297}$

25.
$$\begin{array}{r} \$20.00 \\ 3.71 \\ 4.25 \\ +\ .16 \\ \hline \end{array}$$

26. $9\overline{)107}$

27.
$$\begin{array}{r} 2,354 \\ -781 \\ \hline \end{array}$$

28.
$$\begin{array}{r} \$311.26 \\ +47.98 \\ \hline \end{array}$$

29.
$$\begin{array}{r} 251 \\ \times 28 \\ \hline \end{array}$$

30. $17\overline{)238}$

Test Yourself

C Work each problem carefully and write your answer in the space provided

1.
$$
\begin{array}{r} 17 \\ 24 \\ + 86 \\ \hline \end{array}
$$

2.
$$
\begin{array}{r} 96 \\ - 17 \\ \hline \end{array}
$$

3.
$$
\begin{array}{r} 578 \\ 53 \\ 975 \\ 68 \\ + 4{,}048 \\ \hline \end{array}
$$

4.
$$
\begin{array}{r} 257 \\ \times 86 \\ \hline \end{array}
$$

5. $40\overline{)2{,}208}$

6.
$$
\begin{array}{r} \frac{2}{5} \\ + \frac{1}{5} \\ \hline \end{array}
$$

7.
$$
\begin{array}{r} 235 \\ \times 914 \\ \hline \end{array}
$$

8.
$$
\begin{array}{r} \frac{13}{16} \\ - \frac{7}{16} \\ \hline \end{array}
$$

9. $\frac{3}{5} \times \frac{7}{8} =$

10. $\frac{5}{8} \div \frac{2}{3} =$

11.
$$
\begin{array}{r} \frac{1}{3} \\ + \frac{1}{3} \\ \hline \end{array}
$$

12.
$$
\begin{array}{r} 805 \\ - 613 \\ \hline \end{array}
$$

13.
$$
\begin{array}{r} \frac{3}{4} \\ - \frac{1}{4} \\ \hline \end{array}
$$

14. $\frac{5}{6} \times \frac{2}{15} =$

15. $\frac{3}{8} \times \frac{2}{5} =$

16.
$$
\begin{array}{r} 15 \\ - 6 \\ \hline \end{array}
$$

17.
$$
\begin{array}{r} \$2.05 \\ - 1.78 \\ \hline \end{array}
$$

18.
$$
\begin{array}{r} 5 \\ 8 \\ 2 \\ + 9 \\ \hline \end{array}
$$

19.
$$
\begin{array}{r} 978 \\ \times 301 \\ \hline \end{array}
$$

20. $\frac{1}{2} \times 50 =$

21.
$$
\begin{array}{r} 218 \\ \times 74 \\ \hline \end{array}
$$

22.
$$
\begin{array}{r} \$147.93 \\ 26.96 \\ + 18.03 \\ \hline \end{array}
$$

23.
$$
\begin{array}{r} \$147.93 \\ - 18.63 \\ \hline \end{array}
$$

24.
$$
\begin{array}{r} 4{,}711 \\ + 6{,}777 \\ \hline \end{array}
$$

25. $23\overline{)1{,}148}$

26. $9\overline{)1{,}217}$

27.
$$
\begin{array}{r} \$763.99 \\ + 26.47 \\ \hline \end{array}
$$

28.
$$
\begin{array}{r} \$839.67 \\ - 79.79 \\ \hline \end{array}
$$

29. $\frac{5}{10} \times \frac{2}{5} =$

30. $\frac{5}{8} \times \frac{2}{5} =$

Test Yourself

Test Yourself

D Work each problem on your own paper. Write your answer on the line.

1. Three friends bought these items for a picnic lunch: carrot salad, $1.98; turkey slices, $2.59; hard rolls, $1.79; pickles, $1.10; lemonade, $1.98. How much did they spend? If they gave the clerk a ten–dollar bill, how much change should they receive? _____

2. Mr. Braid earns $240 in 5 days. How much does he earn per day? _____

3. The Woo family's bills for January were as follows: gas, $63.89; rent, $550.00; lights, $42.80; and phone, $35.79. How much did they spend in all? _____

4. Maria bought 4 pounds of ground beef. She used $3\frac{1}{2}$ pounds of it. How much ground beef was left? _____

5. Jason works part–time in a local grocery store. Last week he worked the following hours: Monday, 3 hr.; Tuesday, $5\frac{1}{2}$ hr.; Wednesday, $4\frac{1}{2}$ hr.; Thursday, $6\frac{1}{2}$ hr.; Friday, 5 hr.; and Saturday, 8 hr. He earns $4.50 an hour. How much did he earn last week? _____

6. Ilva's father earns $390 a week. How much will he earn in one year? _____

7. Lisa earned $66 last week and $42 this week after payroll deductions. Does she have enough to buy a tape recorder that costs $94? Would she be able to buy two tapes at $9.95 each as well? _____

8. Mr. Mouet purchased a car costing $10,750. He was allowed $2,950 for his old car. How much more does he have to pay for the car? _____

9. The Suttons took a vacation. Their expenses were as follows: motels, $810.25; gasoline, $201.28; food, $643.00; entertainment, $312.80. How much were their total expenses? They had saved $2,000 for this vacation. How much money do they have left? _____

Understanding Fractions

➤ A fraction is one or more of the equal parts of anything.

Examples: $\frac{1}{2}$ (one–half) of a pound of potatoes

$\frac{2}{3}$ (two–thirds) of a cup of milk

$\frac{1}{5}$ (one–fifth) of a dollar

➤ A fraction has two parts:

The **numerator** (the number above the fraction line) tells how many equal parts are used.

The **denominator** (the number below the fraction line) tells the number of equal parts a whole thing is divided into.

Example: Barry is sharing his melon with Cleo, José, and Paula. He must cut it into 4 equal parts so that each person will receive one–fourth ($\frac{1}{4}$) of the melon. After he gives a piece to Cleo, 3 of the 4 equal parts are left for José, Paula, and himself. Therefore, three–fourths ($\frac{3}{4}$) of the melon is left.

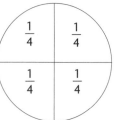

In the fraction $\frac{1}{4}$, the 1 (the number above the fraction line) is the **numerator**; the 4 (the number below the fraction line) is the **denominator.**

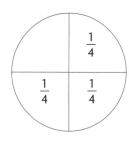

$\frac{1}{4}$ numerator
    denominator

■ Study this diagram:

1. How many equal parts is it divided into? _____

2. How many equal parts are shaded? _____

3. Write the fraction that the diagram shows. _____

Count the number of sections in each diagram. Write the fraction that tells the number of sections that are shaded.

1.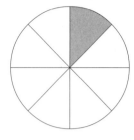

_____

2.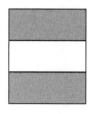

_____

3.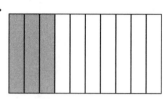

_____

4.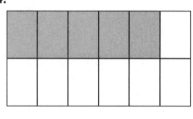

_____

5.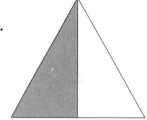

_____

6.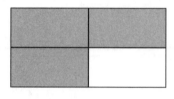

_____

7.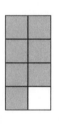

_____

8.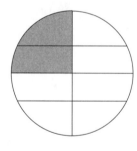

_____

9.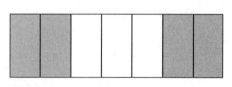

_____

10.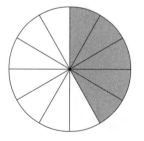

_____

Kinds of Fractions

There are three kinds of fractions. It is important to know these fractions and be able to recognize them.

➤ Proper, or common, fraction—a fraction whose numerator is smaller than its denominator:

Examples: $\frac{1}{2}$ $\frac{7}{9}$ $\frac{1}{4}$ $\frac{5}{8}$ $\frac{13}{15}$

➤ Improper fraction—a fraction in which the numerator is the same size as the denominator, or larger than the denominator.

Examples: $\frac{8}{3}$ $\frac{4}{4}$ $\frac{9}{4}$ $\frac{5}{2}$ $\frac{3}{3}$ $\frac{10}{10}$ $\frac{21}{2}$

➤ Mixed number—a number made of a whole number and a proper fraction.

Examples: $1\frac{1}{4}$ $2\frac{2}{3}$ $5\frac{1}{5}$ $6\frac{1}{2}$ $7\frac{3}{4}$

In the space provided write the kind of fraction each one represents.

Example: $\frac{12}{12}$ improper fraction $\frac{2}{9}$ proper fraction $1\frac{1}{4}$ mixed number

1. $\frac{12}{3}$ _____

2. $1\frac{5}{12}$ _____

3. $\frac{1}{3}$ _____

4. $9\frac{1}{4}$ _____

5. $\frac{36}{5}$ _____

6. $\frac{20}{1}$ _____

7. $\frac{6}{6}$ _____

8. $\frac{3}{2}$ _____

9. $\frac{7}{8}$ _____

10. $1\frac{3}{10}$ _____

11. $\frac{3}{17}$ _____

12. $5\frac{7}{64}$ _____

13. $17\frac{16}{17}$ _____

14. $100\frac{31}{32}$ _____

15. $5\frac{7}{64}$ _____

16. $\frac{57}{64}$ _____

Reducing Fractions to Lowest Terms

A proper fraction can be reduced to lowest terms by dividing the numerator and denominator by the largest number (but not zero or one) that divides evenly into both of them without a remainder. Reducing does not change the value of the fraction.

Example: The diagram on the right shows that $\frac{4}{8}$ of the circle is the same as $\frac{1}{2}$ of the circle: $\frac{4}{8} = \frac{1}{2}$.

We can get $\frac{1}{2}$ by dividing the numerator and denominator by 4.

Therefore:

$$\frac{4}{8} = \frac{\overset{1}{4} \div \overset{1}{4}}{\underset{2}{8} \div \underset{1}{4}} = \frac{1}{2}$$

NOTE: Try dividing the numerator and denominator by the numerator given; if it cannot be divided evenly, count backward, by ones, from the given numerator until you find the largest number that can be divided evenly into both parts.

$\frac{6}{8} = ?$ Can 6 and 8 be divided by 6? **no**
by 5? **no**
by 4? **no**
by 3? **no**
by 2? **yes**

Therefore 2 is the number to use to reduce the fraction.

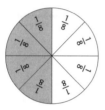
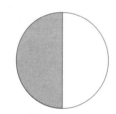

Study these examples.

$$\frac{3}{9} = \frac{3 \div 3}{9 \div 3} = \frac{1}{3} \qquad \frac{30}{36} = \frac{30 \div 6}{36 \div 6} = \frac{5}{6} \qquad \frac{6}{8} = \frac{6 \div 2}{8 \div 2} = \frac{3}{4} \qquad \frac{14}{28} = \frac{14 \div 14}{28 \div 14} = \frac{1}{2}$$

A Reduce each fraction to its lowest terms.

1. $\frac{12}{16} = \frac{12 \div 4}{16 \div 4} = \frac{3}{4}$

2. $\frac{8}{10} =$

3. $\frac{3}{12} =$

4. $\frac{2}{4} =$

5. $\frac{9}{36} =$

6. $\frac{13}{52} =$

7. $\frac{10}{25} =$

8. $\frac{6}{16} =$

9. $\frac{6}{12} =$

10. $\frac{15}{45} =$

11. $\frac{23}{69} =$

12. $\frac{16}{36} =$

13. $\frac{16}{64} =$

14. $\frac{16}{96} =$

15. $\frac{7}{49} =$

16. $\frac{4}{32} =$

B Reduce each fraction to its lowest terms.

1. $\dfrac{4}{16} = \dfrac{4 \div 4}{16 \div 4} = \dfrac{1}{4}$

2. $\dfrac{6}{10} =$

3. $\dfrac{7}{14} =$

4. $\dfrac{9}{18} =$

5. $\dfrac{10}{12} =$

6. $\dfrac{8}{12} =$

7. $\dfrac{21}{27} =$

8. $\dfrac{5}{20} =$

9. $\dfrac{2}{10} =$

10. $\dfrac{3}{18} =$

11. $\dfrac{10}{18} =$

12. $\dfrac{4}{28} =$

13. $\dfrac{4}{22} =$

14. $\dfrac{14}{16} =$

15. $\dfrac{18}{54} =$

16. $\dfrac{30}{32} =$

17. $\dfrac{16}{24} =$

18. $\dfrac{6}{9} =$

19. $\dfrac{12}{20} =$

20. $\dfrac{30}{45} =$

21. $\dfrac{15}{40} =$

22. $\dfrac{22}{40} =$

23. $\dfrac{34}{51} =$

24. $\dfrac{49}{63} =$

25. $\dfrac{36}{54} =$

26. $\dfrac{14}{24} =$

27. $\dfrac{4}{18} =$

28. $\dfrac{20}{25} =$

29. $\dfrac{13}{26} =$

30. $\dfrac{21}{49} =$

31. $\dfrac{11}{77} =$

32. $\dfrac{9}{63} =$

33. $\dfrac{8}{42} =$

34. $\dfrac{6}{16} =$

35. $\dfrac{12}{44} =$

36. $\dfrac{26}{39} =$

37. $\dfrac{25}{35} =$

38. $\dfrac{14}{42} =$

39. $\dfrac{19}{57} =$

40. $\dfrac{9}{12} =$

21

Changing Fractions

To change an improper fraction to a whole number or a mixed number, **divide** the numerator by the denominator.

Study these examples:

$$\frac{11}{4} = 4\overline{)11}\;\;2\frac{3}{4} \qquad \frac{12}{3} = 3\overline{)12}\;\;4 \qquad \frac{5}{3} = 3\overline{)5}\;\;1\frac{2}{3} \qquad \frac{6}{2} = 2\overline{)6}\;\;3$$

A Change each improper fraction to a whole number or a mixed number.

$$\frac{8}{4} = 4\overline{)8}\;\;2$$

1. $\frac{84}{12} =$

2. $\frac{27}{4} =$

3. $\frac{8}{3} =$

4. $\frac{7}{2} =$

5. $\frac{9}{2} =$

6. $\frac{36}{3} =$

7. $\frac{12}{5} =$

8. $\frac{18}{6} =$

9. $\frac{9}{9} =$

10. $\frac{34}{3} =$

11. $\frac{11}{3} =$

12. $\frac{20}{3} =$

13. $\frac{57}{11} =$

14. $\frac{52}{7} =$

15. $\frac{19}{5} =$

16. $\frac{10}{7} =$

17. $\frac{13}{4} =$

18. $\frac{17}{6} =$

B Change each improper fraction to a whole number or a mixed number.

1. $\frac{11}{5} =$

2. $\frac{35}{4} =$

3. $\frac{15}{6} =$

4. $\frac{24}{4} =$

5. $\frac{16}{5} =$

6. $\frac{3}{2} =$

7. $\frac{7}{3} =$

8. $\frac{21}{5} =$

9. $\frac{16}{7} =$

10. $\frac{12}{2} =$

11. $\frac{33}{11} =$

12. $\frac{3}{3} =$

13. $\frac{10}{3} =$

14. $\frac{46}{7} =$

15. $\frac{4}{2} =$

16. $\frac{39}{14} =$

17. $\frac{26}{6} =$

18. $\frac{17}{2} =$

To change a mixed number to an improper fraction, **multiply** the whole number by the denominator of the fraction and then add the numerator to this product. Write the answer over the denominator given.

Look at these examples. Can you explain what was done?

   a. $1\frac{1}{2} = \frac{1 \times 2 + 1}{2} = \frac{3}{2}$ **b.** $3\frac{1}{4} = \frac{3 \times 4 + 1}{4} = \frac{13}{4}$

   c. $3\frac{5}{12} = \frac{3 \times 12 + 5}{12} = \frac{41}{12}$ **d.** $5\frac{3}{8} = \frac{5 \times 8 + 3}{8} = \frac{43}{8}$

C Change each mixed number to an improper fraction.

1. $2\frac{3}{4} =$ 6. $8\frac{2}{9} =$

2. $6\frac{3}{11} =$ 7. $2\frac{1}{4} =$

3. $4\frac{1}{3} =$ 8. $4\frac{3}{5} =$

4. $5\frac{1}{7} =$ 9. $2\frac{3}{10} =$

5. $12\frac{5}{8} =$ 10. $3\frac{2}{5} =$

D Change each mixed number to an improper fraction.

1. $9\frac{4}{11} =$ 6. $1\frac{1}{4} =$

2. $2\frac{1}{3} =$ 7. $5\frac{2}{3} =$

3. $8\frac{4}{9} =$ 8. $7\frac{1}{8} =$

4. $6\frac{1}{2} =$ 9. $8\frac{5}{12} =$

5. $5\frac{7}{8} =$ 10. $4\frac{1}{2} =$

A Write the word or words that will make each of the following sentences true. Use these words:

improper	denominator	mixed
fraction	proper	numerator

1. A(n)_____ is one or more of the equal parts of anything.

2. A(n)_____ fraction is a fraction whose numerator is smaller than the denominator.

3. The_____ tells how many equal parts of a whole thing are used.

4. A(n)_____ fraction is a fraction whose numerator is the same size as or larger than the denominator.

5. The part of the fraction that tells the number of equal parts a whole thing is divided into is called the _____.

6. A(n)_____ number is a fraction made of a whole number and a proper fraction.

B Write the name that each fraction represents.

1. $\frac{15}{5}$ _____

2. $2\frac{1}{2}$ _____

3. $\frac{44}{7}$ _____

4. $\frac{3}{4}$ _____

5. $37\frac{2}{3}$ _____

6. $\frac{14}{10}$ _____

7. $\frac{13}{14}$ _____

8. $13\frac{1}{14}$ _____

9. $\frac{3}{26}$ _____

10. $\frac{31}{26}$ _____

11. $1\frac{9}{10}$ _____

12. $10\frac{1}{9}$ _____

13. $\frac{100}{99}$ _____

14. $\frac{5}{6}$ _____

15. $\frac{2}{13}$ _____

16. $9\frac{1}{8}$ _____

17. $\frac{8}{19}$ _____

18. $\frac{9}{6}$ _____

C Change each mixed number to an improper fraction.

1. $2\frac{7}{8} =$

2. $1\frac{3}{4} =$

3. $6\frac{2}{7} =$

4. $1\frac{5}{6} =$

5. $9\frac{2}{3} =$

6. $8\frac{1}{2} =$

7. $5\frac{1}{12} =$

8. $4\frac{3}{10} =$

9. $2\frac{1}{4} =$

10. $3\frac{3}{8} =$

11. $1\frac{1}{19} =$

12. $2\frac{15}{16} =$

D Change each improper fraction to a whole number or a mixed number.

1. $\frac{20}{4} =$

2. $\frac{8}{7} =$

3. $\frac{75}{7} =$

4. $\frac{5}{2} =$

5. $\frac{125}{8} =$

6. $\frac{63}{9} =$

7. $\frac{63}{8} =$

8. $\frac{68}{17} =$

9. $\frac{37}{2} =$

10. $\frac{100}{27} =$

11. $\frac{81}{9} =$

12. $\frac{91}{13} =$

Adding Like Fractions

Like fractions are fractions whose denominators are the same. To add proper like fractions, add the numerators together and write the sum over the denominator given. If the answer is an improper fraction, change it to a whole number or a mixed number. If the answer is a proper fraction, reduce it to its lowest terms.

Study these examples:

a. $\dfrac{1}{3}$
$+\dfrac{1}{3}$
$\dfrac{2}{3}$

b. $\dfrac{3}{8}$
$+\dfrac{1}{8}$
$\dfrac{4 \div 4}{8 \div 4} = \dfrac{1}{2}$

c. $\dfrac{2}{3}$
$+\dfrac{2}{3}$
$\dfrac{4}{3}$ $= 3\overline{)4}^{\,1\frac{1}{3}}$
$\underline{-3}$
1

d. $\dfrac{1}{2}$
$\dfrac{3}{2}$
$+\dfrac{7}{2}$
$\dfrac{11}{2}$ $= 2\overline{)11}^{\,5\frac{1}{2}}$
$\underline{-10}$
1

A Add these fractions. Reduce or change when possible.

1. $\dfrac{2}{5}$
$+\dfrac{1}{5}$

2. $\dfrac{5}{6}$
$+\dfrac{4}{6}$

3. $\dfrac{3}{8}$
$+\dfrac{1}{8}$

4. $\dfrac{1}{4}$
$+\dfrac{1}{4}$

5. $\dfrac{3}{7}$
$+\dfrac{2}{7}$

6. $\dfrac{2}{15}$
$+\dfrac{8}{15}$

7. $\dfrac{4}{5}$
$+\dfrac{1}{5}$

8. $\dfrac{11}{12}$
$+\dfrac{1}{12}$

9. $\dfrac{3}{4}$
$+\dfrac{2}{4}$

10. $\dfrac{5}{8}$
$+\dfrac{2}{8}$

11. $\dfrac{4}{7}$
$+\dfrac{1}{7}$

12. $\dfrac{1}{16}$
$+\dfrac{3}{16}$

13. $\frac{5}{9}$
$+\frac{1}{9}$
___

14. $\frac{7}{12}$
$+\frac{5}{12}$
___

15. $\frac{1}{2}$
$+\frac{2}{2}$
___

16. $\frac{1}{6}$
$\frac{5}{6}$
$+\frac{2}{6}$
___

To add mixed numbers with like denominators, first add the numerators of the proper fractions. Second, add the whole numbers. Third, if the answer contains an **improper fraction** and a **whole number**, change the answer to an improper fraction. Then, change that to a whole number or a mixed number. If the answer is a proper fraction and a whole number, reduce the proper fraction to its lowest terms.

Study this example:

Margaret worked $2\frac{1}{2}$ hours Monday, $1\frac{1}{2}$ hours Tuesday, and $5\frac{1}{2}$ hours Thursday. How many hours did she work?

The answer contains an improper fraction, $\frac{3}{2}$, and a whole number, 8. Change the answer to an improper fraction.

Therefore, $8\frac{3}{2} = \frac{8 \times 2 + 3}{2} = \frac{19}{2} = 2\overline{)19}^{\,9\frac{1}{2}}$
$\underline{-18}$
1

NOTE:

$2\frac{1}{2}$ means 2 whole hours and $\frac{1}{2}$ of another

$1\frac{1}{2}$ means 1 whole hour and $\frac{1}{2}$ of another

$5\frac{1}{2}$ means 5 whole hours and $\frac{1}{2}$ of another
_____

8 whole hours and $\frac{3}{2} = 8\frac{3}{2}$ hours

Therefore, Margaret worked $9\frac{1}{2}$ hours.

Study these examples. Can you tell how they were added?

a. $1\frac{1}{4}$
$+3\frac{1}{4}$
___
$4\frac{2}{4} = 4\frac{1}{2}$

b. 7
$+\frac{3}{4}$
___
$7\frac{3}{4}$

c. $1\frac{2}{3}$
$+6\frac{1}{3}$
___
$7\frac{3}{3} = \frac{7 \times 3 + 3}{3} = \frac{24}{3} = 3\overline{)24}^{\,8}$
$\phantom{7\frac{3}{3} = \frac{7 \times 3 + 3}{3} = \frac{24}{3} = 3}\underline{-24}$
$\phantom{7\frac{3}{3} = \frac{7 \times 3 + 3}{3} = \frac{24}{3} = 33}0$

B Study item 1, which is done for you. Then do the others. Remember to reduce or change to a whole number or mixed number when possible.

1. $2\frac{3}{4}$
    $+ 6\frac{1}{4}$
    $8\frac{4}{4} = \frac{8 \times 4 + 4}{4} = \frac{36}{4} = 9$

2. $5\frac{6}{7}$
    $+ 1\frac{3}{7}$

3. $7\frac{1}{3}$
    $+ \frac{1}{3}$

4. $4\frac{1}{2}$
    $+ 3\frac{1}{2}$

5. $1\frac{5}{9}$
    $+ 3\frac{4}{9}$

6. $5\frac{3}{4}$
    $+ \frac{3}{4}$

7. $3\frac{1}{4}$
    $+ 5\frac{3}{4}$

8. $6\frac{1}{6}$
    $+ 1\frac{5}{6}$

9. $9\frac{2}{3}$
    $+ 16$

10. $1\frac{1}{5}$
    $+ 7\frac{3}{5}$

11. $3\frac{3}{5}$
    $+ 4\frac{3}{5}$

12. $6\frac{11}{12}$
    $+ 4\frac{1}{12}$

13. $7\frac{3}{8}$
    $+ 2\frac{2}{8}$

14. $9\frac{1}{8}$
    $+ 7\frac{5}{8}$

15. $8\frac{2}{7}$
    $+ 3\frac{6}{7}$

16. $8\frac{1}{2}$
    $+ 5\frac{1}{2}$

17. $3\frac{7}{12}$
    $+ 2\frac{5}{12}$

18. $3\frac{2}{3}$
    $+ 14\frac{2}{3}$

C Add these fractions. Reduce or change to a mixed number or whole number.

1. $9\frac{7}{10}$
   $+ 4\frac{3}{10}$
   _____

2. $16\frac{3}{8}$
   $+ 11\frac{7}{8}$
   _____

3. $18\frac{3}{8}$
   $+ 14\frac{5}{8}$
   _____

4. $7\frac{3}{8}$
   $9\frac{6}{8}$
   $+ 1\frac{4}{8}$
   _____

5. $9\frac{3}{32}$
   $14\frac{6}{32}$
   $+ 2\frac{21}{32}$
   _____

6. $4\frac{15}{32}$
   $2\frac{1}{32}$
   $+ 7$
   _____

7. 13
   $8\frac{5}{16}$
   $+ 26\frac{1}{16}$
   _____

8. $3\frac{1}{2}$
   $12\frac{1}{2}$
   $7\frac{1}{2}$
   $+ 6\frac{1}{2}$
   _____

9. $18\frac{1}{4}$
   $9\frac{3}{4}$
   $10\frac{3}{4}$
   $+ 6\frac{1}{4}$
   _____

10. $\frac{11}{25}$
    $+ 30$
    _____

11. $10\frac{11}{64}$
    $+ 6\frac{25}{64}$
    _____

12. $9\frac{23}{50}$
    $+ 6\frac{17}{50}$
    _____

13. $1\frac{3}{5}$
    $8\frac{1}{5}$
    $+ 6\frac{2}{5}$
    _____

14. $10\frac{1}{16}$
    $3\frac{5}{16}$
    $+ 6\frac{7}{16}$
    _____

15. $8\frac{19}{60}$
    $1\frac{23}{60}$
    $+ 11\frac{14}{60}$
    _____

16. $2\frac{3}{4}$
    $24\frac{3}{4}$
    $+ 9\frac{1}{4}$
    _____

17. $3\frac{11}{100}$
    $+ 2\frac{14}{100}$
    _____

18. $2\frac{9}{10}$
    $+ 45\frac{7}{10}$
    _____

Adding Unlike Fractions

1. **Unlike fractions** are fractions whose denominators are not the same.

2. Before you can add unlike fractions, the denominators must be made the same. In other words, there must be a **common denominator**.

3. A **common denominator** is the smallest number into which each original denominator can be divided evenly without a remainder.

4. To find the smallest, or least, common denominator if it is not the denominator of one of the fractions given:

   a. Take the largest denominator and multiply it by 2, 3, 4, or 5 (and so forth) until you find the smallest number into which each original denominator can be divided evenly.

   b. **Divide** the original denominators into the common denominator.

   c. **Multiply** your answers by the original numerators. You'll have new numerators and denominators.

   d. **Add** the new numerators together, and write the sum over the new denominator. Then add the whole numbers if any are used.

   e. If the answer is
      (1) a proper fraction, reduce it to the lowest terms, if possible.
      (2) an improper fraction, change it to a whole number or a mixed number.
      (3) a whole number and an improper fraction, change it to an improper fraction, and then change it to a whole number or mixed number.

$$\text{a.} \quad \frac{2}{9}\left(\frac{1}{1}\right) = \frac{2}{9}$$
$$+\frac{1}{3}\left(\frac{3}{3}\right) = \frac{3}{9}$$
$$\overline{\quad\quad\quad\quad \frac{5}{9}}$$

Look at example a. The denominators are 9 and 3. Both 9 and 3 can be divided evenly into 9. Therefore, 9 is the least common denominator. The answer is a proper fraction in its lowest terms, so it cannot be reduced further.

Look at example b. Before finding the least common denominator, rewrite the whole numbers. The denominators are 6, 4, and 2. All three cannot be divided evenly into 6. To find the common denominator, multiply 2 x 6. Your answer is 12. All three can be divided evenly into 12; therefore, 12 is the least common denominator. The answer is a whole number and an improper fraction, so it must be changed to an improper fraction and then to a whole number or a mixed number.

$$\text{b.} \quad 3\frac{1}{6}\left(\frac{2}{2}\right) = 3\frac{2}{12}$$
$$6\frac{3}{4}\left(\frac{3}{3}\right) = 6\frac{9}{12}$$
$$+1\frac{1}{2}\left(\frac{6}{6}\right) = 1\frac{6}{12}$$
$$10\frac{17}{12} = \frac{10 \times 12 + 17}{12} = \frac{137}{12} = 12\overline{)137}^{\,11\frac{5}{12}}$$
$$\begin{array}{r} -12 \\ \hline 17 \\ -12 \\ \hline 5 \end{array}$$

Study these examples. Notice how they were added.

a.
$$\frac{1}{2}\left(\frac{2}{2}\right) = \frac{2}{4}$$
$$+\frac{1}{4}\left(\frac{1}{1}\right) = \frac{1}{4}$$
$$\frac{3}{4}$$

b.
$$\frac{1}{4}\left(\frac{2}{2}\right) = \frac{2}{8}$$
$$+\frac{1}{8}\left(\frac{1}{1}\right) = \frac{1}{8}$$
$$\frac{3}{8}$$

c.
$$2\frac{1}{2}\left(\frac{5}{5}\right) = 2\frac{5}{10}$$
$$+3\frac{2}{5}\left(\frac{2}{2}\right) = 3\frac{4}{10}$$
$$5\frac{9}{10}$$

d.
$$1\frac{5}{12}\left(\frac{2}{2}\right) = 1\frac{10}{24}$$

$$2\frac{7}{8}\left(\frac{3}{3}\right) = 2\frac{21}{24}$$

$$+4\frac{1}{4}\left(\frac{6}{6}\right) = 4\frac{6}{24}$$

$$7\frac{37}{24} = \frac{7 \times 24 + 37}{24} = \frac{205}{24} = 24\overline{)205}\,{}^{8\frac{13}{24}}$$
$$-\,192$$
$$13$$

A Study the examples done for you. Then do the others yourself.

1.
$$\frac{7}{8}$$
$$+\frac{3}{4}$$
_____

2.
$$\frac{1}{3}$$
$$+\frac{5}{6}$$
_____

3.
$$\frac{1}{2}$$
$$+\frac{3}{10}$$
_____

4.
$$\frac{2}{9}$$
$$1\frac{1}{2}$$
$$+7\frac{1}{6}$$
_____

5.
$$\frac{1}{12}$$
$$6\frac{1}{2}$$
$$+1\frac{1}{6}$$
_____

6.
$$4\frac{1}{2}$$
$$2\frac{1}{16}$$
$$+\frac{1}{4}$$
_____

7. $\frac{1}{4}$
$4\frac{1}{2}$
$+\,5\frac{1}{5}$

8. $6\frac{1}{3}$
$\frac{1}{4}$
$+\,\frac{1}{2}$

9. $\frac{2}{9}$
$\frac{5}{12}$
$+\,\frac{1}{3}$

10. $1\frac{1}{4}$
$1\frac{1}{6}$
$+\,6\frac{3}{8}$

11. $1\frac{1}{7}$
$+\,1\frac{1}{8}$

12. $2\frac{1}{5}$
$+\,5\frac{1}{4}$

13. $4\frac{2}{3}$
$+\,1\frac{1}{6}$

14. $3\frac{1}{6}$
$4\frac{3}{8}$
$+\,1\frac{1}{2}$

15. $3\frac{1}{5}$
$5\frac{2}{3}$
$+\,2\frac{1}{6}$

B Add these mixed numbers.

1. $2\frac{1}{3}$
$+\,4\frac{1}{2}$

2. $8\frac{3}{5}$
$+\,2\frac{1}{4}$

3. $3\frac{5}{6}$
$+\,2\frac{2}{3}$

4. $6\frac{1}{2}$
$3\frac{1}{4}$
$+\,5\frac{5}{8}$

5. $7\frac{1}{3}$
$2\frac{6}{7}$
$+\,1\frac{8}{9}$

6. $3\frac{1}{3}$
$2\frac{1}{4}$
$+\,2\frac{5}{6}$

7. $8\frac{5}{16}$
$9\frac{7}{8}$
$+\,7$

8. $7\frac{1}{8}$
$9\frac{2}{5}$
$+\,5\frac{3}{4}$

9. $1\frac{1}{2}$
$1\frac{3}{4}$
$+\,1\frac{1}{3}$

C Add these fractions.

1. $\frac{1}{3}$
    $+\frac{1}{2}$

2. $2\frac{1}{3}$
    $+1\frac{1}{4}$

3. $\frac{2}{3}$
    $\frac{1}{4}$
    $+\frac{1}{6}$

4. $\frac{5}{6}$
    $\frac{1}{2}$
    $+\frac{1}{3}$

5. $1\frac{1}{2}$
    $2\frac{3}{5}$
    $+2\frac{7}{10}$

6. $3\frac{1}{12}$
    $4\frac{3}{4}$
    $+2\frac{1}{8}$

7. $3\frac{1}{9}$
    $1\frac{1}{6}$
    $+2\frac{1}{3}$

8. $3\frac{1}{7}$
    $+4\frac{1}{4}$

9. $7\frac{5}{6}$
    $+6\frac{4}{7}$

10. $9\frac{3}{8}$
    $+1\frac{3}{6}$

11. $9\frac{2}{3}$
    $+6\frac{1}{12}$

12. $5\frac{3}{4}$
    $+8\frac{1}{5}$

13. $7\frac{1}{6}$
    $2\frac{3}{8}$
    $+9\frac{1}{8}$

14. $4\frac{2}{5}$
    $+1\frac{3}{7}$

15. $7\frac{2}{3}$
    $+8\frac{3}{4}$

16. $\frac{5}{6}$
    $+3\frac{7}{8}$

Review

A Change to a whole number
or a mixed number.

1. $\dfrac{18}{12} =$

6. $\dfrac{7}{5} =$

2. $\dfrac{16}{16} =$

7. $\dfrac{20}{4} =$

3. $\dfrac{9}{8} =$

8. $\dfrac{32}{8} =$

4. $\dfrac{12}{6} =$

9. $\dfrac{33}{8} =$

5. $\dfrac{4}{3} =$

10. $\dfrac{9}{6} =$

B Reduce these fractions to lowest terms.

1. $\dfrac{8}{10} =$

6. $\dfrac{10}{15} =$

2. $\dfrac{2}{4} =$

7. $\dfrac{4}{6} =$

3. $\dfrac{12}{16} =$

8. $\dfrac{3}{12} =$

4. $\dfrac{2}{8} =$

9. $\dfrac{6}{16} =$

5. $\dfrac{5}{15} =$

10. $\dfrac{4}{8} =$

C Change to an improper fraction.

1. $1\dfrac{1}{2} =$

2. $1\dfrac{3}{5} =$

3. $5\dfrac{1}{8} =$

4. $5\dfrac{1}{4} =$

5. $3\dfrac{1}{3} =$

6. $2\dfrac{5}{6} =$

7. $3\dfrac{2}{7} =$

8. $9\dfrac{1}{9} =$

9. $1\dfrac{1}{6} =$

D Add these fractions.

1. $\begin{array}{r} \frac{2}{5} \\ + \frac{1}{5} \\ \hline \end{array}$

2. $\begin{array}{r} \frac{1}{3} \\ + \frac{1}{3} \\ \hline \end{array}$

3. $\begin{array}{r} \frac{3}{8} \\ + \frac{1}{8} \\ \hline \end{array}$

4. $\begin{array}{r} 12\frac{3}{8} \\ + 2\frac{5}{6} \\ \hline \end{array}$

5. $\begin{array}{r} \frac{3}{7} \\ + \frac{2}{7} \\ \hline \end{array}$

6. $\begin{array}{r} 5\frac{3}{4} \\ + \frac{7}{16} \\ \hline \end{array}$

7. $\begin{array}{r} 19\frac{1}{2} \\ + 4\frac{1}{7} \\ \hline \end{array}$

8. $\begin{array}{r} 6\frac{1}{9} \\ + 9\frac{5}{6} \\ \hline \end{array}$

9. $\begin{array}{r} 6\frac{2}{3} \\ + 5\frac{1}{6} \\ \hline \end{array}$

10. $\begin{array}{r} 19\frac{1}{9} \\ + 3\frac{2}{3} \\ \hline \end{array}$

11. $\begin{array}{r} 10\frac{5}{6} \\ + 7\frac{5}{8} \\ \hline \end{array}$

12. $\begin{array}{r} 13 \\ 8\frac{5}{16} \\ + 26\frac{1}{8} \\ \hline \end{array}$

13. $\begin{array}{r} 2\frac{3}{4} \\ 6\frac{1}{4} \\ + 2\frac{1}{4} \\ \hline \end{array}$

14. $\begin{array}{r} 6\frac{3}{4} \\ 7\frac{1}{4} \\ + 6\frac{1}{3} \\ \hline \end{array}$

15. $\begin{array}{r} 7\frac{3}{4} \\ 1\frac{5}{12} \\ + 1\frac{5}{7} \\ \hline \end{array}$

16. $\begin{array}{r} 12 \\ + 9\frac{1}{8} \\ \hline \end{array}$

17. $\begin{array}{r} 6\frac{3}{11} \\ 14\frac{9}{11} \\ + 9\frac{3}{4} \\ \hline \end{array}$

18. $\begin{array}{r} 2\frac{3}{16} \\ 4\frac{7}{8} \\ + 9\frac{2}{7} \\ \hline \end{array}$

19. $\begin{array}{r} 1\frac{5}{14} \\ 6\frac{3}{14} \\ + 7\frac{1}{4} \\ \hline \end{array}$

20. $\begin{array}{r} 3\frac{2}{3} \\ + 4\frac{3}{4} \\ \hline \end{array}$

21. $\begin{array}{r} 2\frac{1}{2} \\ 5\frac{1}{8} \\ + 7\frac{1}{4} \\ \hline \end{array}$

22. $\begin{array}{r} 1\frac{1}{3} \\ 2\frac{5}{8} \\ + 1\frac{5}{6} \\ \hline \end{array}$

23. $\begin{array}{r} 7\frac{1}{3} \\ 3\frac{1}{5} \\ + 6\frac{5}{6} \\ \hline \end{array}$

24. $\begin{array}{r} 1\frac{5}{6} \\ 3\frac{5}{9} \\ + 2\frac{2}{3} \\ \hline \end{array}$

25. $\begin{array}{r} 25\frac{1}{2} \\ 5\frac{1}{3} \\ + 4\frac{3}{5} \\ \hline \end{array}$

26. $\begin{array}{r} 1\frac{5}{8} \\ 1\frac{7}{12} \\ + 1\frac{5}{6} \\ \hline \end{array}$

27. $\begin{array}{r} 3\frac{1}{4} \\ 3\frac{1}{8} \\ + 3\frac{1}{2} \\ \hline \end{array}$

28. $\begin{array}{r} 9\frac{3}{4} \\ 4\frac{5}{7} \\ + 1\frac{1}{4} \\ \hline \end{array}$

Subtracting Like Fractions

Like fractions are fractions whose denominators are the same.

To subtract like fractions, first subtract the numerators and write the answer over the denominator given.

Example: To subtract $\frac{1}{5}$ from $\frac{3}{5}$, subtract the 1 from the 3, leaving $\frac{2}{5}$.

$$\begin{array}{r} \frac{3}{5} \\ -\frac{1}{5} \\ \hline \frac{2}{5} \end{array}$$

Study these examples. Notice how they were subtracted.

a. $\begin{array}{r} \frac{7}{8} \\ -\frac{5}{8} \\ \hline \frac{2}{8} = \frac{1}{4} \end{array}$

b. $\begin{array}{r} 2\frac{3}{4} \\ -1\frac{1}{4} \\ \hline 1\frac{2}{4} = 1\frac{1}{2} \end{array}$

c. $\begin{array}{r} 8\frac{2}{3} \\ -2\frac{2}{3} \\ \hline 6 \end{array}$

d. $\begin{array}{r} 3\frac{5}{6} \\ -1 \\ \hline 2\frac{5}{6} \end{array}$

A Subtract these fractions and mixed numbers. Reduce when possible.

1. $\begin{array}{r} 7\frac{1}{2} \\ -\frac{1}{2} \\ \hline \end{array}$
   $\begin{array}{r} 2\frac{1}{3} \\ -1\frac{1}{3} \\ \hline \end{array}$
   $\begin{array}{r} \frac{11}{12} \\ -\frac{5}{12} \\ \hline \end{array}$
   $\begin{array}{r} 10\frac{7}{8} \\ -6\frac{5}{8} \\ \hline \end{array}$

2. $\begin{array}{r} 2\frac{3}{4} \\ -\frac{1}{4} \\ \hline \end{array}$
   $\begin{array}{r} 14\frac{5}{8} \\ -8\frac{3}{8} \\ \hline \end{array}$
   $\begin{array}{r} 7\frac{9}{16} \\ -\frac{5}{16} \\ \hline \end{array}$
   $\begin{array}{r} 3\frac{6}{7} \\ -1\frac{4}{7} \\ \hline \end{array}$

3. $\begin{array}{r} 4\frac{2}{3} \\ -1\frac{1}{3} \\ \hline \end{array}$
   $\begin{array}{r} 2\frac{1}{2} \\ -\frac{1}{2} \\ \hline \end{array}$
   $\begin{array}{r} 3\frac{3}{8} \\ -\frac{1}{8} \\ \hline \end{array}$
   $\begin{array}{r} 5\frac{7}{12} \\ -2\frac{5}{12} \\ \hline \end{array}$

Sometimes a subtraction problem contains **no fraction on the top,** or the **fraction below is larger** than the one above. Then it is necessary to borrow from the whole number on top. You borrow 1 from this number.

Example: Inez had 3 yards of mailing tape. She used $\frac{5}{8}$ yards to seal several envelopes.

SOLUTION: Since you cannot subtract $\frac{5}{8}$ from nothing, borrow 1 from 3, leaving 2. The 1 stands for a whole thing, but equals 8 eighths, so 8 becomes the denominator in the fraction $2\frac{8}{8}$ as shown. Now you can subtract. The check shows the answer is right.

$$3 = 2\frac{8}{8}$$
$$-\frac{5}{8} = \frac{5}{8}$$
$$2\frac{3}{8}$$

Check

$$2\frac{3}{8}$$
$$+\frac{5}{8}$$
$$2\frac{8}{8} = \frac{2 \times 8 + 8}{8} = \frac{24}{8} = 8\overline{)24}\ \ {}^{3}$$
$$-24$$
$$0$$

Example: Oscar had $8\frac{1}{8}$ pounds of flour. He used $3\frac{5}{8}$ pounds to prepare some noodles. How much flour does he have left?

SOLUTION: Although these are like fractions, you cannot subtract them, because the bottom fraction is larger. Borrow 1 from the 8, leaving 7. The borrowed 1 contains 8 eighths, so you can add the top numerators together and write the answer over the denominator given: $8 + 1 = \frac{9}{8}$. Rewrite the bottom number.

Now you can subtract.

$$8\frac{1}{8} = 7\frac{9}{8}$$
$$-3\frac{5}{8} = 3\frac{5}{8}$$
$$4\frac{4}{8}$$

Check

$$4\frac{4}{8}$$
$$+3\frac{5}{8}$$
$$7\frac{9}{8} = \frac{7 \times 8 + 9}{8} = \frac{65}{8} = 8\overline{)65}\ \ {}^{8\frac{1}{8}}$$
$$-64$$
$$1$$

Study these examples. Notice how they were subtracted.

a.

$$5\frac{1}{3} = 4\frac{4}{3}$$
$$-3\frac{2}{3} = 3\frac{2}{3}$$
$$1\frac{2}{3}$$

Check

$$1\frac{2}{3}$$
$$+3\frac{2}{3}$$
$$4\frac{4}{3} = \frac{4 \times 3 + 4}{3} = \frac{16}{3} = 3\overline{)16}\ \ {}^{5\frac{1}{3}}$$
$$-15$$
$$1$$

b. $6\frac{1}{16} = 5\frac{17}{16}$

$-\frac{5}{16} = \frac{5}{16}$

$5\frac{12}{16} = 5\frac{3}{4}$

Check

$5\frac{12}{16}$

$+\frac{5}{16}$

$5\frac{17}{16} = \frac{5 \times 16 + 17}{16} = \frac{97}{16} = 16\overline{)97}\,^{6\frac{1}{16}}$

$\underline{-\ 96}$

1

c. $4 = 3\frac{6}{6}$

$-1\frac{5}{6} = 1\frac{5}{6}$

$2\frac{1}{6}$

Check

$2\frac{1}{6}$

$+1\frac{5}{6}$

$3\frac{6}{6} = \frac{3 \times 6 + 6}{6} = \frac{24}{6} = 6\overline{)24}\,^{4}$

$\underline{-\ 24}$

0

d. $1 = \frac{3}{3}$

$-\frac{2}{3} = \frac{2}{3}$

$\frac{1}{3}$

Check

$\frac{1}{3}$

$+\frac{2}{3}$

$\frac{3}{3} = \frac{1}{3\overline{)3}}$

$\underline{-\ 3}$

0

B Study each example and do the other problems.
Check your answers.

1. $4\frac{7}{12}$

$-\frac{11}{12}$

_____

Check

2. $8\frac{2}{5}$

$-2\frac{4}{5}$

_____

Check

3. $5\frac{1}{3}$

$-3\frac{2}{3}$

_____

Check

Example:

$$2 = 1\frac{10}{10}$$
$$-1\frac{7}{10} = 1\frac{7}{10}$$
$$\frac{3}{10}$$

Check

$$\frac{3}{10}$$
$$+1\frac{7}{10}$$
$$1\frac{10}{10} = \frac{1 \times 10 + 10}{10} = \frac{20}{10} = 10\overline{)20}$$
$$-20$$
$$0$$

with quotient 2

4. $\quad 6$

$\quad -\dfrac{3}{4}$

Check

5. $\quad 8$

$\quad -4\dfrac{2}{3}$

Check

6. $\quad 3$

$\quad -1\dfrac{1}{2}$

Check

7. $\quad 7\dfrac{1}{4}$

$\quad -2\dfrac{3}{4}$

Check

C Subtract these fractions. Check your answers.

Check

1.   4

    $- 1\frac{5}{6}$

    _____

Check

2. $6\frac{1}{4}$

    $- 2\frac{3}{4}$

    _____

Check

3. $11\frac{1}{5}$

    $- 7\frac{3}{5}$

    _____

Check

4.   3

    $- \frac{1}{8}$

    _____

Check

5. $9\frac{1}{6}$

    $- \frac{5}{6}$

    _____

Check

6.   8

    $- \frac{1}{16}$

    _____

7. $6\frac{3}{16}$
$-3\frac{5}{16}$

Check

8. $10\frac{5}{8}$
$-1\frac{7}{8}$

Check

9. $9\frac{3}{5}$
$-2\frac{4}{5}$

Check

10. $9\frac{3}{7}$
$-2\frac{4}{7}$

Check

11. $7\frac{5}{8}$
$-\frac{7}{8}$

Check

12. $1\frac{1}{16}$
$-\frac{15}{16}$

Check

Subtracting Unlike Fractions **Lesson 8**

Unlike fractions are fractions whose denominators are not the same. To subtract unlike fractions, do the following:

1. Write the whole numbers.

2. Find the least common denominator. (The least common denominator is the smallest number into which each original denominator can be divided evenly.)

3. Borrow 1 from the whole number on the top if the bottom fraction is larger than the top fraction.

4. Add the numerator and denominator of the top fraction, and write the answer over the common denominator.

Example: Esther bought $7\frac{1}{4}$ pounds of ground beef for a cookout. She used $5\frac{7}{8}$ pounds of it. How much ground beef did she have left?

SOLUTION: First, write the whole numbers. Find the common denominator. The common denominator for 8 and 4 is 8. Then divide each original denominator into 8 and multiply the answer times the numerator to get new ones. The top fraction is smaller than the bottom fraction, so borrow 1 from 7 leaving 6. Then add the top fraction together and write the answer over the 8 because 8 is the common denominator $(8 + 2 = \frac{10}{8})$. Bring over the bottom whole number and fraction.
Now subtract.

$$7\frac{1}{4}\left(\frac{2}{2}\right) = 7\frac{2}{8} = 6\frac{10}{8}$$
$$-5\frac{7}{8}\left(\frac{2}{2}\right) = 5\frac{7}{8} = 5\frac{7}{8}$$
$$1\frac{3}{8}$$

Check

$$1\frac{3}{8}$$
$$+5\frac{7}{8}$$
$$6\frac{10}{8} = \frac{6 \times 8 + 10}{8} = \frac{58}{8} = 8\overline{)58} \quad 7\frac{2}{8} = 7\frac{1}{4}$$
$$\underline{-56}$$
$$2$$

Study these examples. Notice how they were subtracted.

a.
$$4\frac{3}{4}\left(\frac{3}{3}\right) = 4\frac{9}{12}$$
$$-2\frac{2}{3}\left(\frac{4}{4}\right) = 2\frac{8}{12}$$
$$2\frac{1}{12}$$

Check

$$2\frac{1}{12}$$
$$+2\frac{8}{12}$$
$$4\frac{9}{12} = 4\frac{3}{4}$$

b. $5\frac{2}{9}\left(\frac{1}{1}\right) = 5\frac{2}{9} = 4\frac{11}{9}$

$\underline{-2\frac{1}{3}\left(\frac{3}{3}\right) = 2\frac{3}{9} = 2\frac{3}{9}}$

$\phantom{-2\frac{1}{3}\left(\frac{3}{3}\right) = 2\frac{3}{9} = }\ 2\frac{8}{9}$

Check $2\frac{8}{9}$

$\underline{+2\frac{3}{9}}$

$4\frac{11}{9} = \frac{4 \times 9 + 11}{9} = \frac{47}{9} = 9\overline{)47}\,^{5\frac{2}{9}}$

$\phantom{4\frac{11}{9} = \frac{4 \times 9 + 11}{9} = \frac{47}{9} = 9\overline{)}}\underline{-45}$

$\phantom{4\frac{11}{9} = \frac{4 \times 9 + 11}{9} = \frac{47}{9} = 9\overline{)47}}2$

c. $4\frac{1}{8}\left(\frac{1}{1}\right) = 4\frac{1}{8} = 3\frac{9}{8}$

$\underline{-1\frac{1}{4}\left(\frac{2}{2}\right) = 1\frac{2}{8} = 1\frac{2}{8}}$

$\phantom{-1\frac{1}{4}\left(\frac{2}{2}\right) = 1\frac{2}{8} = }\ 2\frac{7}{8}$

Check $2\frac{7}{8}$

$\underline{+1\frac{2}{8}}$

$3\frac{9}{8} = \frac{3 \times 8 + 9}{8} = \frac{33}{8} = 8\overline{)33}\,^{4\frac{1}{8}}$

$\phantom{3\frac{9}{8} = \frac{3 \times 8 + 9}{8} = \frac{33}{8} = 8\overline{)}}\underline{-32}$

$\phantom{3\frac{9}{8} = \frac{3 \times 8 + 9}{8} = \frac{33}{8} = 8\overline{)33}}1$

d. $9\frac{3}{5}\left(\frac{2}{2}\right) = 9\frac{6}{10}$

$\underline{-8\frac{3}{10}\left(\frac{1}{1}\right) = 8\frac{3}{10}}$

$\phantom{-8\frac{3}{10}\left(\frac{1}{1}\right) = }\ 1\frac{3}{10}$

Check $1\frac{3}{10}$

$\underline{+8\frac{3}{10}}$

$9\frac{6}{10} = 9\frac{3}{5}$

A Study the examples. Then subtract and check the others yourself.

1.
$6\frac{1}{12}$
$\underline{-3\frac{1}{6}}$

Check

2.
$10\frac{1}{2}$
$\underline{-2\frac{7}{8}}$

Check

3.
$5\frac{1}{8}$
$\underline{-\frac{3}{4}}$

Check

4. $12\frac{5}{16}$

   $-\ 8\frac{3}{4}$
   _____

Check

5. $5\frac{1}{3}$

   $-\ 3\frac{2}{6}$
   _____

Check

6. $6\frac{3}{4}$

   $-\ 3\frac{7}{8}$
   _____

Check

7. $2\frac{5}{9}$

   $-\ \frac{2}{3}$
   _____

Check

8. $6\frac{3}{4}$

   $-\ 1\frac{7}{8}$
   _____

Check

9. $5\frac{1}{4}$

   $-\ 2\frac{5}{6}$
   _____

Check

10. $2\frac{1}{2}$

   $-\ 1\frac{2}{3}$
   _____

Check

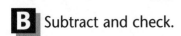

B Subtract and check.

1. $7\frac{1}{2}$ **Check**

   $-4\frac{1}{6}$

2. $8\frac{3}{4}$ **Check**

   $-2\frac{1}{5}$

3. $4\frac{1}{2}$ **Check**

   $-1\frac{3}{8}$

4. $8\frac{3}{10}$ **Check**

   $-3\frac{3}{4}$

5. $9\frac{1}{4}$ **Check**

   $-\frac{5}{6}$

6. $6\frac{1}{3}$ **Check**

   $-4\frac{3}{7}$

7. $7\frac{3}{4}$ **Check**

   $-1\frac{7}{8}$

8. $3\frac{4}{5}$ **Check**

   $-1\frac{5}{6}$

C Subtract and check.

1.
$$9\frac{5}{12}$$
$$-\ 4\frac{1}{4}$$

Check

5.
$$1\frac{5}{6}$$
$$-\ \frac{1}{3}$$

Check

2.
$$4\frac{3}{8}$$
$$-\ 3\frac{3}{4}$$

Check

6.
$$7\frac{5}{7}$$
$$-\ 3\frac{1}{2}$$

Check

3.
$$3\frac{1}{6}$$
$$-\ \frac{4}{9}$$

Check

7.
$$3\frac{1}{2}$$
$$-\ 2\frac{3}{4}$$

Check

4.
$$3\frac{1}{4}$$
$$-\ 1\frac{5}{8}$$

Check

8.
$$19\frac{2}{3}$$
$$-\ 1\frac{5}{6}$$

Check

A Reduce these proper fractions to lowest terms.

1. $\dfrac{16}{64} =$

2. $\dfrac{4}{14} =$

3. $\dfrac{13}{39} =$

4. $\dfrac{3}{6} =$

5. $\dfrac{30}{32} =$

6. $\dfrac{3}{15} =$

7. $\dfrac{9}{33} =$

8. $\dfrac{9}{12} =$

9. $\dfrac{8}{12} =$

10. $\dfrac{16}{20} =$

11. $\dfrac{5}{20} =$

12. $\dfrac{15}{60} =$

B Change to a whole number or to a mixed number.

1. $\dfrac{8}{8} =$

2. $\dfrac{11}{5} =$

3. $\dfrac{13}{8} =$

4. $\dfrac{17}{3} =$

5. $\dfrac{4}{2} =$

6. $\dfrac{40}{13} =$

7. $\dfrac{9}{4} =$

8. $\dfrac{48}{12} =$

9. $\dfrac{6}{5} =$

10. $\dfrac{18}{16} =$

11. $\dfrac{11}{4} =$

12. $\dfrac{18}{6} =$

C Change to improper fractions.

1. $1\frac{1}{3} =$

2. $2\frac{1}{5} =$

3. $2\frac{1}{2} =$

4. $3\frac{1}{8} =$

5. $1\frac{1}{4} =$

6. $2\frac{2}{9} =$

7. $1\frac{2}{7} =$

8. $2\frac{1}{6} =$

9. $1\frac{7}{8} =$

10. $10\frac{2}{3} =$

D Add these fractions.

1.
$$\frac{1}{3}$$
$$+ \frac{1}{3}$$

2.
$$\frac{1}{2}$$
$$+ \frac{1}{4}$$

3.
$$5\frac{3}{8}$$
$$+ 1\frac{3}{4}$$

4.
$$\frac{4}{5}$$
$$+ \frac{2}{5}$$

5.
$$5\frac{3}{4}$$
$$+ 7\frac{2}{3}$$

6.
$$7\frac{1}{16}$$
$$+ 2\frac{1}{8}$$

7.
$$1\frac{3}{4}$$
$$+ 3\frac{5}{8}$$

8.
$$3\frac{1}{6}$$
$$+ 1\frac{2}{3}$$

9.
$$6\frac{5}{6}$$
$$+ 1\frac{4}{7}$$

10.
$$\frac{3}{4}$$
$$+ \frac{5}{8}$$

E Subtract and check these fractions.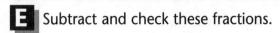

1. $6\frac{1}{2}$ **Check**

    $-\frac{1}{2}$

2. $9\frac{4}{5}$ **Check**

    $-\frac{3}{5}$

3. $1\frac{1}{4}$ **Check**

    $-\frac{1}{2}$

4. $6\frac{1}{2}$ **Check**

    $-3\frac{1}{6}$

5. $9\frac{1}{4}$ **Check**

    $-3\frac{7}{8}$

6. $7\frac{1}{7}$ **Check**

    $-2\frac{1}{2}$

7. $1\frac{2}{7}$ **Check**

    $-\frac{3}{5}$

8. $3\frac{1}{3}$ **Check**

    $-1\frac{3}{4}$

9. $4\frac{3}{8}$ **Check**

    $-2\frac{5}{6}$

10. $3\frac{2}{3}$ **Check**

    $-1\frac{5}{6}$

Multiplying Fractions

Lesson 9

To multiply proper fractions, first multiply the numerators straight across, and then the denominators straight across. If your answer is an improper fraction, change it to a whole number or a mixed number.

Examples:

a. $\dfrac{7}{8} \times \dfrac{4}{5} = \dfrac{28}{40}$

b. $\dfrac{2}{3} \times \dfrac{1}{4} = \dfrac{2}{12}$

c. $\dfrac{4}{5} \times \dfrac{1}{3} = \dfrac{4}{15}$

A Study the examples. Then do items 1 to 3.

1. $\dfrac{1}{6} \times \dfrac{1}{2} =$

2. $\dfrac{1}{2} \times \dfrac{3}{4} =$

3. $\dfrac{5}{6} \times \dfrac{1}{2} =$

B Multiply these fractions.

1. $\dfrac{1}{2} \times \dfrac{5}{8} =$

2. $\dfrac{7}{8} \times \dfrac{1}{2} =$

3. $\dfrac{9}{10} \times \dfrac{3}{8} =$

4. $\dfrac{1}{3} \times \dfrac{5}{8} =$

5. $\dfrac{4}{9} \times \dfrac{2}{9} =$

6. $\dfrac{2}{3} \times \dfrac{3}{15} =$

7. $\dfrac{3}{5} \times \dfrac{5}{6} =$

8. $\dfrac{1}{4} \times \dfrac{3}{4} =$

9. $\dfrac{1}{3} \times \dfrac{5}{9} =$

10. $\dfrac{1}{12} \times \dfrac{1}{3} =$

11. $\dfrac{1}{5} \times \dfrac{1}{10} =$

12. $\dfrac{1}{3} \times \dfrac{3}{4} =$

13. $\dfrac{1}{2} \times \dfrac{1}{2} =$

14. $\dfrac{5}{6} \times \dfrac{6}{7} =$

15. $\dfrac{2}{9} \times \dfrac{3}{8} =$

16. $\dfrac{4}{7} \times \dfrac{4}{11} =$

C Multiply these fractions.

1. $\frac{1}{2} \times \frac{1}{7} =$

2. $\frac{1}{3} \times \frac{1}{5} =$

3. $\frac{1}{2} \times \frac{1}{3} =$

4. $\frac{1}{4} \times \frac{1}{8} =$

5. $\frac{1}{9} \times \frac{1}{10} =$

6. $\frac{3}{9} \times \frac{2}{9} =$

7. $\frac{1}{7} \times \frac{1}{8} =$

8. $\frac{3}{11} \times \frac{1}{2} =$

9. $\frac{2}{3} \times \frac{3}{5} =$

10. $\frac{5}{7} \times \frac{5}{6} =$

11. $\frac{3}{8} \times \frac{2}{9} =$

12. $\frac{2}{7} \times \frac{5}{8} =$

13. $\frac{5}{9} \times \frac{2}{3} =$

14. $\frac{1}{5} \times \frac{1}{4} =$

15. $\frac{3}{4} \times \frac{7}{10} =$

16. $\frac{2}{3} \times \frac{9}{16} =$

17. $\frac{1}{2} \times \frac{4}{5} =$

18. $\frac{5}{6} \times \frac{4}{9} =$

19. $\frac{2}{3} \times \frac{2}{7} =$

20. $\frac{3}{10} \times \frac{1}{3} =$

21. $\frac{2}{3} \times \frac{1}{2} =$

22. $\frac{6}{7} \times \frac{7}{8} =$

23. $\frac{3}{5} \times \frac{5}{9} =$

24. $\frac{7}{11} \times \frac{1}{2} =$

D Multiply these fractions.

1. $\frac{1}{6} \times \frac{1}{2} =$

2. $\frac{5}{6} \times \frac{1}{2} =$

3. $\frac{4}{5} \times \frac{1}{2} =$

4. $\frac{2}{3} \times \frac{3}{7} =$

5. $\frac{1}{8} \times \frac{1}{2} =$

6. $\frac{1}{3} \times \frac{1}{2} =$

7. $\frac{2}{5} \times \frac{1}{12} =$

8. $\frac{5}{9} \times \frac{1}{2} =$

9. $\frac{1}{5} \times \frac{2}{7} =$

10. $\frac{1}{13} \times \frac{1}{2} =$

11. $\frac{1}{6} \times \frac{3}{5} =$

12. $\frac{1}{2} \times \frac{2}{5} =$

13. $\frac{3}{4} \times \frac{5}{6} =$

14. $\frac{1}{3} \times \frac{4}{5} =$

15. $\frac{3}{10} \times \frac{5}{6} =$

16. $\frac{2}{5} \times \frac{3}{8} =$

17. $\frac{7}{8} \times \frac{4}{5} =$

18. $\frac{1}{4} \times \frac{1}{2} =$

19. $\frac{2}{5} \times \frac{9}{5} =$

20. $\frac{3}{8} \times \frac{1}{3} =$

21. $\frac{1}{2} \times \frac{1}{32} =$

22. $\frac{3}{10} \times \frac{1}{5} =$

23. $\frac{7}{8} \times \frac{1}{8} =$

24. $\frac{3}{16} \times \frac{1}{2} =$

Multiplying Fractions and Whole Numbers

To multiply fractions and whole numbers, first change the whole number to a fraction. Then multiply the numerators straight across. Then multiply the denominators straight across. The denominator of a whole number is the number 1. If your answer is an improper fraction, change it to a whole number or a mixed number. Simplify your answer to lowest terms.

Study these examples. Notice how they were multiplied.

a. $\quad \dfrac{1}{3} \times 18 = \dfrac{1 \times 18}{3 \times 1} = \dfrac{18}{3} = 3\overline{)18}$ with quotient 6, -18, 0

b. $\quad 5 \times \dfrac{3}{8} = \dfrac{5 \times 3}{1 \times 8} = \dfrac{15}{8} = 8\overline{)15}$ with quotient $1\frac{7}{8}$, -8, 7

c. $\quad 9 \times \dfrac{3}{9} = \dfrac{9 \times 3}{1 \times 9} = \dfrac{27}{9} = 9\overline{)27}$ with quotient 3, -27, 0

d. $\quad \dfrac{1}{3} \times 12 = \dfrac{1 \times 12}{3 \times 1} = \dfrac{12}{3} = 3\overline{)12}$ with quotient 4, -12, 0

e. $\quad 2 \times \dfrac{1}{9} = \dfrac{2 \times 1}{1 \times 9} = \dfrac{2}{9}$

A Multiply these fractions and whole numbers. If your answer is an improper fraction, change it to a whole number or a mixed number. Simplify your answers.

1. $\frac{1}{2} \times 3 =$

2. $5 \times \frac{2}{3} =$

3. $9 \times \frac{2}{7} =$

4. $\frac{4}{9} \times 9 =$

5. $\frac{2}{3} \times 6 =$

6. $5 \times \frac{3}{5} =$

7. $3 \times \frac{1}{9} =$

8. $\frac{6}{7} \times 4 =$

9. $\frac{1}{11} \times 10 =$

10. $\frac{1}{10} \times 20 =$

11. $9 \times \frac{2}{3} =$

12. $8 \times \frac{1}{4} =$

13. $\frac{1}{4} \times 16 =$

14. $\frac{5}{6} \times 18 =$

15. $\frac{2}{3} \times 12 =$

16. $\frac{4}{5} \times 8 =$

17. $\frac{5}{6} \times 9 =$

18. $\frac{5}{9} \times 12 =$

19. $13 \times \frac{1}{4} =$

20. $\frac{3}{7} \times 4 =$

21. $7 \times \frac{1}{8} =$

22. $26 \times \frac{3}{7} =$

23. $\frac{1}{12} \times 5 =$

24. $8 \times \frac{7}{8} =$

B Multiply these fractions and whole numbers. If your answer is an improper fraction, change it to a whole number or a mixed number. Simplify your answers.

1. $\frac{3}{4} \times 40 =$

2. $\frac{1}{4} \times 2 =$

3. $12 \times \frac{3}{8} =$

4. $\frac{8}{9} \times 3 =$

5. $\frac{1}{5} \times 45 =$

6. $\frac{7}{8} \times 3 =$

7. $4 \times \frac{3}{4} =$

8. $16 \times \frac{2}{7} =$

9. $\frac{5}{6} \times 14 =$

10. $12 \times \frac{1}{9} =$

11. $6 \times \frac{3}{4} =$

12. $\frac{4}{5} \times 30 =$

13. $\frac{2}{3} \times 9 =$

14. $36 \times \frac{5}{6} =$

15. $\frac{2}{5} \times 25 =$

16. $10 \times \frac{1}{13} =$

17. $\frac{2}{7} \times 19 =$

18. $3 \times \frac{11}{32} =$

19. $\frac{3}{7} \times 9 =$

20. $\frac{3}{16} \times 7 =$

21. $\frac{3}{16} \times 8 =$

22. $\frac{3}{14} \times 8 =$

23. $6 \times \frac{5}{6} =$

24. $\frac{5}{16} \times 13 =$

NOTE: The examples show two ways to find the answer. The examples *a, b,* and *c* show two ways of finding the same answer. In examples *a* and *c* the answers are found, and then the fractions are reduced to their lowest terms. In examples *b* and *d,* both the **numerators** and **denominators** are divided evenly by the same number or numbers. In example *b* the number is 3, and in example *d* the numbers are 2 and 3. This process is called **cancellation**. Then the numerators and denominators are multiplied. Because of the cancellation, answers *b* and *d* are already in lowest terms.

a.
$$24 \times \frac{8}{15} = \frac{24 \times 8}{1 \times 15} = \frac{192}{15} = 15\overline{)192}$$
$$\frac{12\frac{12}{15} = 12\frac{4}{5}}{}$$
$$-15$$
$$42$$
$$-30$$
$$12$$

c.
$$\frac{2}{3} \times \frac{3}{12} = \frac{6}{36} = \frac{1}{6}$$

b.
$$24 \times \frac{8}{15} = \frac{24 \times \overset{8}{8}}{1 \times \cancel{15}_5} = \frac{64}{5} = 5\overline{)64}$$
$$12\frac{4}{5}$$
$$-5$$
$$14$$
$$-10$$
$$4$$

d.
$$\frac{\overset{1}{\cancel{2}}}{\cancel{3}_1} \times \frac{\overset{1}{\cancel{3}}}{\cancel{12}_6} = \frac{1}{6}$$

Study the following examples. Notice how they were multiplied.

a.
$$\frac{5}{6} \times \frac{4}{5} = \frac{20}{30} = \frac{2}{3}$$

c.
$$\frac{1}{3} \times 18 = \frac{1 \times 18}{3 \times 1} = \frac{18}{3} = 3\overline{)18}$$
$$\frac{6}{}$$
$$-18$$
$$0$$

$$\frac{\overset{1}{\cancel{5}}}{\cancel{6}_3} \times \frac{\overset{2}{\cancel{4}}}{\cancel{5}_1} = \frac{2}{3}$$

$$\frac{1}{3} \times 18 = \frac{1 \times \overset{6}{\cancel{18}}}{\cancel{3}_1 \times 1} = \frac{6}{1} = 1\overline{)6}$$
$$\frac{6}{}$$
$$-6$$
$$0$$

b.
$$2 \times \frac{1}{4} = \frac{2 \times 1}{1 \times 4} = \frac{2}{4} = \frac{1}{2}$$

$$2 \times \frac{1}{4} = \frac{\overset{1}{\cancel{2}} \times 1}{1 \times \cancel{4}_2} = \frac{1}{2}$$

A Multiply. Cancel when you can. Remember to divide the numerator and denominator by the same number.

1. $21 \times \dfrac{2}{3} =$

2. $\dfrac{3}{5} \times 12 =$

3. $9 \times \dfrac{2}{3} =$

4. $\dfrac{2}{9} \times 36 =$

5. $\dfrac{1}{3} \times \dfrac{3}{8} =$

6. $\dfrac{5}{14} \times \dfrac{7}{8} =$

7. $\dfrac{1}{5} \times \dfrac{1}{2} =$

8. $\dfrac{4}{5} \times 15 =$

9. $\dfrac{4}{20} \times \dfrac{25}{32} =$

10. $100 \times \dfrac{1}{10} =$

11. $\dfrac{3}{36} \times \dfrac{6}{18} =$

12. $28 \times \dfrac{4}{7} =$

13. $\dfrac{3}{4} \times 16 =$

14. $\dfrac{2}{3} \times \dfrac{2}{5} =$

15. $20 \times \dfrac{1}{4} =$

16. $9 \times \dfrac{5}{6} =$

17. $\dfrac{5}{8} \times 15 =$

18. $\dfrac{4}{9} \times \dfrac{3}{20} =$

19. $\dfrac{1}{4} \times \dfrac{1}{8} =$

20. $24 \times \dfrac{3}{4} =$

21. $\dfrac{6}{35} \times \dfrac{14}{15} =$

22. $\dfrac{3}{4} \times \dfrac{24}{33} =$

23. $\dfrac{18}{36} \times \dfrac{3}{6} =$

24. $\dfrac{5}{6} \times 25 =$

B Multiply. Cancel when you can.

1. $\dfrac{3}{4} \times 4 =$

2. $\dfrac{2}{7} \times \dfrac{5}{8} =$

3. $\dfrac{2}{3} \times \dfrac{5}{6} =$

4. $\dfrac{7}{8} \times 48 =$

5. $8 \times \dfrac{2}{3} =$

6. $3 \times \dfrac{3}{8} =$

7. $\dfrac{5}{7} \times \dfrac{4}{5} =$

8. $\dfrac{1}{2} \times 10 =$

9. $\dfrac{5}{6} \times 42 =$

10. $6 \times \dfrac{4}{15} =$

11. $42 \times \dfrac{6}{7} =$

12. $\dfrac{7}{16} \times \dfrac{1}{8} =$

13. $2 \times \dfrac{5}{6} =$

14. $\dfrac{1}{8} \times 16 =$

15. $\dfrac{2}{3} \times \dfrac{3}{4} =$

16. $15 \times \dfrac{2}{9} =$

17. $\dfrac{2}{3} \times \dfrac{5}{9} =$

18. $\dfrac{1}{6} \times 18 =$

19. $\dfrac{5}{13} \times \dfrac{13}{25} =$

20. $\dfrac{3}{4} \times \dfrac{8}{15} =$

21. $13 \times \dfrac{3}{39} =$

22. $24 \times \dfrac{3}{4} =$

23. $\dfrac{3}{13} \times \dfrac{1}{26} =$

24. $18 \times \dfrac{3}{8} =$

C Change to an improper fraction.

1. $7\frac{1}{5} =$

2. $5\frac{1}{3} =$

3. $12\frac{1}{2} =$

4. $1\frac{3}{4} =$

5. $7\frac{1}{6} =$

6. $10\frac{2}{3} =$

7. $5\frac{1}{6} =$

8. $7\frac{1}{8} =$

9. $8\frac{1}{9} =$

10. $9\frac{1}{8} =$

11. $2\frac{3}{7} =$

12. $8\frac{2}{5} =$

13. $10\frac{1}{5} =$

14. $2\frac{1}{12} =$

15. $3\frac{1}{15} =$

16. $8\frac{1}{2} =$

17. $4\frac{2}{9} =$

18. $6\frac{2}{3} =$

19. $2\frac{1}{5} =$

20. $11\frac{1}{4} =$

21. $9\frac{2}{5} =$

22. $4\frac{3}{8} =$

23. $1\frac{15}{16} =$

24. $3\frac{1}{4} =$

25. $8\frac{5}{6} =$

26. $6\frac{5}{8} =$

27. $5\frac{7}{8} =$

28. $12\frac{1}{4} =$

29. $16\frac{1}{2} =$

30. $7\frac{3}{10} =$

31. $3\frac{6}{7} =$

32. $1\frac{11}{32} =$

33. $6\frac{3}{4} =$

34. $2\frac{2}{3} =$

35. $4\frac{5}{11} =$

36. $17\frac{1}{2} =$

37. $6\frac{5}{9} =$

38. $3\frac{2}{9} =$

39. $13\frac{1}{3} =$

40. $7\frac{3}{4} =$

41. $5\frac{2}{5} =$

42. $2\frac{5}{7} =$

43. $3\frac{2}{13} =$

44. $8\frac{1}{6} =$

45. $6\frac{1}{6} =$

Multiplying Mixed Numbers

To multiply mixed numbers, first change the mixed number to an improper fraction. Then multiply the same way you multiply proper fractions.

Study these examples. Notice how they are multiplied.

a. $8 \times 1\frac{1}{4} = \frac{8 \times 5}{1 \times 4} = \frac{40}{4} = 4\overline{)40}^{\,10}$

$\begin{array}{r} -4 \\ \hline 00 \\ -00 \\ \hline 0 \end{array}$

c. $5\frac{2}{3} \times 9 = \frac{17 \times 9}{3 \times 1} = \frac{153}{3} = 3\overline{)153}^{\,51}$

$\begin{array}{r} -15 \\ \hline 3 \\ -3 \\ \hline 0 \end{array}$

$8 \times 1\frac{1}{4} = \frac{\overset{2}{\cancel{8}} \times 5}{\cancel{1 \times 4}} = \frac{10}{1} = 1\overline{)10}^{\,10}$

$\begin{array}{r} -1 \\ \hline 00 \\ -00 \\ \hline 0 \end{array}$

$5\frac{2}{3} \times 9 = \frac{17 \times \overset{3}{\cancel{9}}}{\underset{1}{\cancel{3}} \times 1} = \frac{51}{1} = 1\overline{)51}^{\,51}$

$\begin{array}{r} -5 \\ \hline 1 \\ -1 \\ \hline 0 \end{array}$

b. $\frac{3}{4} \times 2\frac{1}{6} = \frac{3 \times 13}{4 \times 6} = \frac{39}{24} =$

d. $4\frac{1}{2} \times \frac{3}{5} = \frac{9 \times 3}{2 \times 5} = \frac{27}{10} = 10\overline{)27}^{\,2\frac{7}{10}}$

$\begin{array}{r} -20 \\ \hline 7 \end{array}$

$\frac{3}{4} \times 2\frac{1}{6} = \frac{\overset{1}{\cancel{3}} \times 13}{4 \times \underset{2}{\cancel{6}}} = \frac{13}{8} = 8\overline{)13}^{\,1\frac{5}{8}}$

$\begin{array}{r} -8 \\ \hline 5 \end{array}$

e. $4\frac{2}{3} \times 3\frac{3}{4} = \frac{\overset{7}{\cancel{14}} \times \overset{5}{\cancel{15}}}{\underset{1}{\cancel{3}} \times \underset{2}{\cancel{4}}} = \frac{35}{2} = 2\overline{)35}^{\,17\frac{1}{2}}$

$\begin{array}{r} -2 \\ \hline 15 \\ -14 \\ \hline 1 \end{array}$

A Multiply these fractions. Cancel when you can.

1. $5\frac{1}{3} \times 4 =$

2. $2\frac{5}{8} \times 1\frac{1}{7} =$

3. $\frac{1}{3} \times 3\frac{2}{3} =$

4. $3\frac{3}{4} \times 2\frac{2}{3} =$

5. $5\frac{2}{3} \times 4\frac{1}{2} =$

6. $1\frac{1}{5} \times 2\frac{1}{4} =$

7. $2\frac{5}{6} \times 3\frac{1}{3} =$

8. $6 \times 4\frac{1}{2} =$

9. $5\frac{1}{4} \times 1\frac{3}{7} =$

10. $2\frac{5}{8} \times 3\frac{2}{3} =$

11. $6\frac{2}{3} \times 4\frac{2}{3} =$

12. $\frac{7}{10} \times 1\frac{5}{6} =$

13. $2\frac{1}{3} \times 1\frac{1}{3} =$

14. $1\frac{4}{5} \times 2\frac{5}{9} =$

15. $2\frac{1}{3} \times 3\frac{1}{7} =$

16. $3 \times 5\frac{3}{4} =$

B Multiply. Cancel when you can.

Example:
$$\frac{2}{3} \times 7\frac{1}{2} = \frac{\overset{1}{\cancel{2}} \times \overset{5}{\cancel{15}}}{\underset{1}{\cancel{3}} \times \underset{1}{\cancel{2}}} = \frac{5}{1} = 1\overline{)5}\quad \begin{array}{r} -5 \\ \hline 0 \end{array}$$

1. $3\frac{1}{2} \times 4 =$

2. $5\frac{1}{7} \times 2\frac{4}{9} =$

3. $\frac{5}{8} \times \frac{7}{10} =$

4. $6\frac{1}{4} \times 2\frac{2}{5} =$

5. $1\frac{2}{5} \times \frac{3}{4} =$

6. $3\frac{3}{5} \times 1\frac{2}{3} =$

7. $3\frac{3}{5} \times 1\frac{2}{3} =$

8. $4 \times 2\frac{1}{6} =$

9. $2\frac{2}{7} \times 8\frac{3}{4} =$

10. $\frac{3}{8} \times 5\frac{1}{3} =$

C Multiply. Cancel when you can.

1. $2\frac{1}{2} \times \frac{2}{5} =$

2. $1\frac{3}{8} \times 6\frac{2}{5} =$

3. $5\frac{5}{9} \times 4\frac{4}{5} =$

4. $5\frac{1}{4} \times 20 =$

5. $2\frac{2}{9} \times 3\frac{1}{10} =$

6. $8\frac{3}{4} \times 1\frac{5}{7} =$

7. $1\frac{4}{5} \times \frac{4}{9} =$

8. $8 \times 2\frac{3}{10} =$

9. $4\frac{2}{7} \times 4\frac{2}{3} =$

10. $8\frac{3}{4} \times 1\frac{1}{7} =$

Review

 Add, subtract, or multiply the fractions.

1. $2\frac{1}{4} \times \frac{2}{3} =$

2. $\frac{7}{8} \times 3\frac{1}{5} =$

3. $6\frac{1}{4}$
   $+ \frac{7}{8}$
   ___

4. $1\frac{2}{3} \times 5\frac{1}{4} =$

5. $\frac{3}{10} \times \frac{5}{8} =$

6. $20\frac{3}{4}$
   $- 12$
   ___

7. $3\frac{1}{6} \times 8 =$

8. $12\frac{1}{4}$
   $+ 18$
   ___

9. $6\frac{1}{4} \times 4\frac{4}{5} =$

10. $9 \times \frac{2}{3} =$

11. $\frac{3}{5} \times \frac{4}{7} =$

12. $15\frac{3}{4}$
    $- 8\frac{7}{8}$
    ___

13. $8\frac{3}{16}$
    $- 5\frac{7}{16}$
    ___

14. $24 \times 1\frac{2}{3} =$

15. $\frac{4}{5} \times \frac{3}{16} =$

16. $6\frac{1}{4}$
    $- 3\frac{7}{16}$
    ___

UNIT 1

To divide fractions, first change the division sign to a times sign. Then **invert** (switch numerator and denominator) the **divisor** (second fraction). Last, multiply the same way you multiply proper fractions.

Study these examples. Notice how they were divided.

a. $\dfrac{2}{3} \div \dfrac{3}{5} = \dfrac{2 \times 5}{3 \times 3} = \dfrac{10}{9} = 9\overline{)10}\,^{1\frac{1}{9}} \quad \dfrac{-\ 9}{\ 1}$

e. $\dfrac{5}{8} \div \dfrac{1}{2} = \dfrac{5 \times 2}{8 \times 1} = \dfrac{10}{8} = \dfrac{5}{4} = 4\overline{)5}\,^{1\frac{1}{4}} \quad \dfrac{-\ 4}{\ 1}$

b. $\dfrac{1}{3} \div \dfrac{1}{2} = \dfrac{1 \times 2}{3 \times 1} = \dfrac{2}{3}$

f. $\dfrac{5}{8} \div \dfrac{1}{2} = \dfrac{5 \times \cancel{2}^{\,1}}{\cancel{8}_{\,2} \times 1} = \dfrac{5}{4} = 4\overline{)5}\,^{1\frac{1}{4}} \quad \dfrac{-\ 4}{\ 1}$

c. $\dfrac{1}{2} \div \dfrac{5}{8} = \dfrac{1 \times 8}{2 \times 5} = \dfrac{8}{10} = \dfrac{4}{5}$

g. $\dfrac{3}{4} \div \dfrac{7}{8} = \dfrac{3 \times \cancel{8}^{\,2}}{\cancel{4}_{\,1} \times 7} = \dfrac{6}{7}$

d. $\dfrac{1}{2} \div \dfrac{5}{8} = \dfrac{1 \times \cancel{8}^{\,4}}{\cancel{2}_{\,1} \times 5} = \dfrac{4}{5}$

Study the examples.

a. $\dfrac{7}{8} \div \dfrac{1}{32} = \dfrac{7 \times \overset{4}{\cancel{32}}}{\underset{1}{\cancel{8}} \times 1} = \dfrac{28}{1} = 1\overline{)28}$

$\dfrac{-2}{8}$
$\dfrac{-8}{0}$

b. $\dfrac{5}{9} \div \dfrac{1}{4} = \dfrac{5 \times 4}{9 \times 1} = \dfrac{20}{9} = 9\overline{)20}^{\,2\frac{2}{9}}$

$\dfrac{-18}{2}$

A Divide these fractions. Cancel when you can.

1. $\dfrac{7}{10} \div \dfrac{2}{3} =$

2. $\dfrac{1}{8} \div \dfrac{1}{5} =$

3. $\dfrac{5}{6} \div \dfrac{1}{3} =$

4. $\dfrac{3}{5} \div \dfrac{1}{2} =$

5. $\dfrac{4}{7} \div \dfrac{6}{7} =$

6. $\dfrac{7}{9} \div \dfrac{1}{7} =$

7. $\dfrac{3}{11} \div \dfrac{2}{3} =$

8. $\dfrac{5}{12} \div \dfrac{5}{36} =$

9. $\dfrac{3}{28} \div \dfrac{3}{49} =$

10. $\dfrac{5}{12} \div \dfrac{3}{4} =$

11. $\dfrac{7}{32} \div \dfrac{5}{64} =$

12. $\dfrac{2}{15} \div \dfrac{2}{3} =$

B Divide. Cancel when you can.

1. $\frac{1}{2} \div \frac{1}{2} =$

2. $\frac{5}{16} \div \frac{1}{3} =$

3. $\frac{5}{8} \div \frac{3}{4} =$

4. $\frac{2}{3} \div \frac{1}{2} =$

5. $\frac{3}{16} \div \frac{1}{5} =$

6. $\frac{7}{8} \div \frac{3}{4} =$

7. $\frac{11}{12} \div \frac{7}{8} =$

8. $\frac{3}{5} \div \frac{12}{25} =$

9. $\frac{12}{25} \div \frac{3}{5} =$

10. $\frac{2}{3} \div \frac{8}{9} =$

11. $\frac{3}{13} \div \frac{5}{39} =$

12. $\frac{2}{5} \div \frac{4}{25} =$

13. $\frac{1}{9} \div \frac{3}{9} =$

14. $\frac{5}{64} \div \frac{5}{8} =$

15. $\frac{9}{10} \div \frac{3}{4} =$

16. $\frac{7}{16} \div \frac{7}{32} =$

C Divide. Cancel when you can.

1. $\dfrac{7}{8} \div \dfrac{2}{5} =$

2. $\dfrac{5}{6} \div \dfrac{1}{5} =$

3. $\dfrac{3}{4} \div \dfrac{1}{3} =$

4. $\dfrac{1}{5} \div \dfrac{1}{4} =$

5. $\dfrac{2}{5} \div \dfrac{1}{10} =$

6. $\dfrac{5}{6} \div \dfrac{3}{10} =$

7. $\dfrac{7}{16} \div \dfrac{1}{7} =$

8. $\dfrac{3}{8} \div \dfrac{3}{10} =$

9. $\dfrac{2}{5} \div \dfrac{7}{8} =$

10. $\dfrac{4}{5} \div \dfrac{5}{6} =$

11. $\dfrac{5}{12} \div \dfrac{4}{5} =$

12. $\dfrac{5}{8} \div \dfrac{1}{4} =$

13. $\dfrac{1}{5} \div \dfrac{2}{15} =$

14. $\dfrac{7}{10} \div \dfrac{3}{5} =$

15. $\dfrac{3}{7} \div \dfrac{3}{8} =$

16. $\dfrac{4}{5} \div \dfrac{2}{5} =$

D Divide. Cancel when you can.

1. $\dfrac{3}{8} \div \dfrac{3}{5} =$

2. $\dfrac{1}{4} \div \dfrac{5}{8} =$

3. $\dfrac{1}{2} \div \dfrac{1}{6} =$

4. $\dfrac{5}{16} \div \dfrac{5}{6} =$

5. $\dfrac{2}{3} \div \dfrac{3}{5} =$

6. $\dfrac{10}{11} \div \dfrac{5}{16} =$

7. $\dfrac{2}{5} \div \dfrac{1}{2} =$

8. $\dfrac{7}{9} \div \dfrac{8}{81} =$

9. $\dfrac{2}{7} \div \dfrac{6}{7} =$

10. $\dfrac{1}{2} \div \dfrac{7}{10} =$

11. $\dfrac{4}{7} \div \dfrac{5}{6} =$

12. $\dfrac{2}{5} \div \dfrac{4}{15} =$

13. $\dfrac{3}{4} \div \dfrac{1}{16} =$

14. $\dfrac{5}{6} \div \dfrac{5}{16} =$

15. $\dfrac{5}{39} \div \dfrac{1}{13} =$

16. $\dfrac{11}{16} \div \dfrac{1}{2} =$

17. $\dfrac{17}{48} \div \dfrac{17}{32} =$

18. $\dfrac{3}{14} \div \dfrac{9}{7} =$

19. $\dfrac{7}{9} \div \dfrac{14}{15} =$

20. $\dfrac{7}{10} \div \dfrac{3}{4} =$

Dividing Fractions and Whole Numbers

To divide fractions and whole numbers, first change the division sign to a times sign. Next, write the number 1 as the denominator of all the whole numbers. Then, invert (write upside down) the divisor (second fraction). Last, multiply the same way that you multiply proper fractions.

Study these examples. Notice how they are divided.

a. $\dfrac{1}{2} \div 6 = \dfrac{1}{2} \div \dfrac{6}{1} = \dfrac{1 \times 1}{2 \times 6} = \dfrac{1}{12}$

b. $\dfrac{5}{6} \div 3 = \dfrac{5}{6} \div \dfrac{3}{1} = \dfrac{5 \times 1}{6 \times 3} = \dfrac{5}{18}$

c. $10 \div \dfrac{5}{6} = \dfrac{10}{1} \div \dfrac{5}{6} = \dfrac{10 \times 6}{1 \times 5} = \dfrac{60}{5} = 5\overline{)60}$ with quotient 12

$$\begin{array}{r} 12 \\ 5\overline{)60} \\ -5 \\ \hline 10 \\ -10 \\ \hline 0 \end{array}$$

or

$$\dfrac{\overset{2}{10} \times 6}{1 \times \underset{1}{5}} = \dfrac{12}{1} = 1\overline{)12}$$

$$\begin{array}{r} 12 \\ 1\overline{)12} \\ -1 \\ \hline 2 \\ -2 \\ \hline 0 \end{array}$$

d. $2 \div \dfrac{1}{4} = \dfrac{2}{1} \div \dfrac{1}{4} = \dfrac{2 \times 4}{1 \times 1} = \dfrac{8}{1} = 1\overline{)8}$

$$\begin{array}{r} 8 \\ 1\overline{)8} \\ -8 \\ \hline 0 \end{array}$$

A Divide. Remember that the denominator of a whole number is 1. Cancel when possible.

1. $\frac{1}{4} \div 3 =$

2. $4 \div \frac{1}{3} =$

3. $\frac{3}{8} \div 5 =$

4. $20 \div \frac{5}{6} =$

5. $\frac{7}{10} \div 6 =$

6. $7 \div \frac{3}{10} =$

B Divide. Cancel when possible.

Examples:

a. $\frac{4}{5} \div 4 = \frac{4}{5} \div \frac{4}{1} = \frac{4 \times 1}{5 \times 4} = \frac{1}{5}$

b. $5 \div \frac{1}{5} = \frac{5}{1} \div \frac{1}{5} = \frac{5 \times 5}{1 \times 1} = \frac{25}{1} = 1\overline{)25}$
$$\begin{array}{r} 25 \\ 1\overline{)25} \\ -2 \\ \hline 5 \\ -5 \\ \hline 0 \end{array}$$

1. $27 \div \frac{3}{5} =$

2. $5 \div \frac{2}{3} =$

3. $\frac{3}{8} \div 2 =$

4. $6 \div \frac{1}{5} =$

5. $\frac{3}{5} \div 27 =$

6. $12 \div \frac{7}{8} =$

7. $4 \div \frac{3}{16} =$

8. $\frac{9}{10} \div 15 =$

C Divide. Cancel when possible.

1. $2 \div \dfrac{1}{10} =$

2. $10 \div \dfrac{1}{5} =$

3. $24 \div \dfrac{3}{4} =$

4. $\dfrac{1}{2} \div 5 =$

5. $3 \div \dfrac{1}{4} =$

6. $\dfrac{7}{10} \div 3 =$

7. $9 \div \dfrac{3}{4} =$

8. $\dfrac{4}{5} \div 14 =$

9. $\dfrac{4}{5} \div 3 =$

10. $13 \div \dfrac{7}{8} =$

11. $10 \div \dfrac{2}{5} =$

12. $\dfrac{3}{5} \div 15 =$

13. $\dfrac{7}{8} \div 7 =$

14. $1 \div \dfrac{3}{16} =$

15. $\dfrac{9}{16} \div 2 =$

16. $\dfrac{3}{4} \div 5 =$

17. $1 \div \dfrac{15}{32} =$

18. $6 \div \dfrac{3}{4} =$

19. $\dfrac{9}{10} \div 4 =$

20. $4 \div \dfrac{9}{10} =$

D Divide. Cancel when you can.

1. $5 \div \dfrac{2}{5} =$

2. $\dfrac{2}{3} \div 2 =$

3. $\dfrac{5}{8} \div 3 =$

4. $9 \div \dfrac{1}{3} =$

5. $\dfrac{3}{8} \div 6 =$

6. $7 \div \dfrac{3}{5} =$

7. $8 \div \dfrac{1}{2} =$

8. $2 \div \dfrac{1}{8} =$

9. $6 \div \dfrac{3}{5} =$

10. $\dfrac{3}{5} \div 6 =$

11. $\dfrac{3}{5} \div 15 =$

12. $12 \div \dfrac{1}{4} =$

13. $5 \div \dfrac{5}{8} =$

14. $6 \div \dfrac{9}{16} =$

15. $\dfrac{8}{9} \div 4 =$

16. $7 \div \dfrac{3}{7} =$

17. $\dfrac{1}{4} \div 8 =$

18. $\dfrac{7}{8} \div 3 =$

19. $5 \div \dfrac{5}{6} =$

20. $\dfrac{7}{8} \div 4 =$

E Divide to find the answer.

1. $\dfrac{3}{4} \div \dfrac{1}{4} =$

2. $10 \div \dfrac{1}{6} =$

3. $\dfrac{1}{4} \div 9 =$

4. $\dfrac{3}{8} \div 2 =$

5. $\dfrac{7}{8} \div \dfrac{1}{16} =$

6. $5 \div \dfrac{1}{3} =$

7. $\dfrac{8}{9} \div 32 =$

8. $\dfrac{5}{6} \div 5 =$

9. $\dfrac{5}{6} \div \dfrac{1}{10} =$

10. $\dfrac{2}{3} \div \dfrac{1}{2} =$

11. $\dfrac{9}{16} \div 3 =$

12. $\dfrac{1}{2} \div \dfrac{1}{4} =$

13. $9 \div \dfrac{3}{4} =$

14. $4 \div \dfrac{5}{6} =$

15. $\dfrac{5}{6} \div 3 =$

16. $7 \div \dfrac{1}{8} =$

17. $6 \div \dfrac{3}{8} =$

18. $\dfrac{4}{15} \div 16 =$

19. $7 \div \dfrac{7}{16} =$

20. $\dfrac{7}{10} \div \dfrac{9}{10} =$

21. $\dfrac{2}{3} \div 4 =$

22. $\dfrac{15}{16} \div 5 =$

23. $\dfrac{1}{4} \div 2 =$

24. $8 \div \dfrac{7}{8} =$

25. $\dfrac{5}{8} \div 4 =$

26. $\dfrac{5}{6} \div 10 =$

27. $\dfrac{5}{9} \div 15 =$

28. $\dfrac{11}{12} \div 22 =$

29. $\dfrac{5}{6} \div 20 =$

30. $\dfrac{3}{4} \div 9 =$

Dividing Mixed Numbers

To divide mixed numbers, first change each mixed number to an improper fraction. Then, change the division sign to a times sign. Next, invert (reverse the numerator and denominator) the divisor (second fraction). Last, multiply the same way that you multiply proper fractions. Use the number 1 as the denominator for all whole numbers.

Study these examples.

a. $2\frac{2}{3} \div \frac{1}{6} = \frac{8}{3} \div \frac{1}{6} = \frac{8 \times 6}{3 \times 1} = \frac{48}{3} = 3\overline{)48}$ give 16 -3 / 18 / -18 / 0 or $\frac{8 \times \overset{2}{6}}{\underset{1}{3} \times 1} = \frac{16}{1} = 1\overline{)16}$ 16 -1 / 6 / -6 / 0

b. $\frac{9}{10} \div 1\frac{4}{5} = \frac{9}{10} \div \frac{9}{5} = \frac{9 \times 5}{10 \times 9} = \frac{45}{90} = \frac{1}{2}$ or $\frac{\overset{1}{9} \times \overset{1}{5}}{\underset{2}{10} \times \underset{1}{9}} = \frac{1}{2}$

c. $1\frac{1}{8} \div 4 = \frac{9}{8} \div \frac{4}{1} = \frac{9 \times 1}{8 \times 4} = \frac{9}{32}$

d. $20 \div 2\frac{1}{4} = \frac{20}{1} \div \frac{9}{4} = \frac{20 \times 4}{1 \times 9} = \frac{80}{9} = 9\overline{)80}$ $8\frac{8}{9}$ -72 / 8

e. $4\frac{1}{2} \div 1\frac{1}{2} = \frac{9}{2} \div \frac{3}{2} = \frac{9 \times 2}{2 \times 3} = \frac{18}{6} = 6\overline{)18}$ 3 -18 / 0 or $\frac{\overset{3}{9} \times \overset{1}{2}}{\underset{1}{2} \times \underset{1}{3}} = \frac{3}{1} = 1\overline{)3}$ 3 -3 / 0

A Study these examples. Then try the others yourself.
Cancel if you can.

a. $4\frac{1}{2} \div \frac{1}{2} = \frac{9}{2} \div \frac{1}{2} = \frac{9 \times 2}{2 \times 1} = \frac{18}{2} = 2\overline{)18} \quad$ or $\quad \frac{9 \times \overset{1}{\cancel{2}}}{\underset{1}{\cancel{2}} \times 1} = \frac{9}{1} = 1\overline{)9}$

$$\begin{array}{r} 9 \\ 2\overline{)18} \\ -18 \\ \hline 0 \end{array} \qquad \begin{array}{r} 9 \\ 1\overline{)9} \\ -9 \\ \hline 0 \end{array}$$

b. $7 \div 2\frac{1}{3} = \frac{7}{1} \div \frac{7}{3} = \frac{7 \times 3}{1 \times 7} = \frac{21}{7} = \quad$ or $\quad \frac{\overset{1}{\cancel{7}} \times 3}{1 \times \underset{1}{\cancel{7}}} = \frac{3}{1} = 1\overline{)3}$

$$\begin{array}{r} 3 \\ 7\overline{)21} \\ -21 \\ \hline 0 \end{array} \qquad \begin{array}{r} 3 \\ 1\overline{)3} \\ -3 \\ \hline 0 \end{array}$$

1. $2\frac{1}{3} \div 1\frac{1}{2} =$

2. $1\frac{1}{2} \div \frac{3}{4} =$

3. $10 \div 1\frac{3}{5} =$

4. $\frac{1}{4} \div 2\frac{1}{2} =$

5. $1\frac{3}{5} \div 2\frac{1}{2} =$

6. $2\frac{1}{2} \div 1\frac{3}{5} =$

7. $1\frac{3}{4} \div 1\frac{2}{3} =$

8. $3\frac{1}{4} \div 1\frac{1}{4} =$

B Divide. Cancel when you can.

1. $4\frac{1}{2} \div \frac{3}{4} =$

2. $4\frac{3}{4} \div 1\frac{1}{8} =$

3. $16 \div 2\frac{4}{5} =$

4. $3\frac{1}{3} \div 1\frac{2}{3} =$

5. $1\frac{1}{2} \div \frac{1}{2} =$

6. $3\frac{1}{3} \div 1\frac{1}{6} =$

7. $5 \div 2\frac{1}{2} =$

8. $2\frac{1}{4} \div 1\frac{1}{8} =$

9. $3\frac{3}{5} \div \frac{3}{5} =$

10. $5\frac{1}{4} \div \frac{1}{8} =$

 **Divide. Cancel when you can.**

1. $3\frac{1}{2} \div 1\frac{1}{2} =$

2. $1\frac{1}{4} \div 3\frac{1}{4} =$

3. $2\frac{3}{4} \div 4 =$

4. $1\frac{3}{8} \div 1\frac{1}{8} =$

5. $8 \div 1\frac{1}{3} =$

6. $2\frac{1}{8} \div 5 =$

7. $\frac{5}{8} \div 2\frac{1}{2} =$

8. $5 \div 2\frac{1}{8} =$

9. $4\frac{1}{5} \div 2\frac{4}{5} =$

10. $2\frac{1}{5} \div 4\frac{4}{5} =$

Divide the fractions.

1. $2\frac{1}{2} \div 1\frac{1}{4} =$

2. $\frac{1}{8} \div \frac{5}{8} =$

3. $\frac{1}{4} \div 9 =$

4. $\frac{7}{9} \div 1\frac{5}{9} =$

5. $1\frac{3}{4} \div 1\frac{2}{3} =$

6. $14 \div \frac{8}{9} =$

7. $\frac{4}{5} \div 6 =$

8. $2\frac{4}{5} \div 2\frac{1}{7} =$

9. $5\frac{1}{7} \div \frac{9}{10} =$

10. $18 \div \frac{6}{7} =$

11. $\frac{9}{10} \div 27 =$

12. $27 \div \frac{9}{10} =$

Changing Fractions to Decimals Lesson 1

To change a fraction to a decimal, first place a decimal point (.) after the numerator and add zeroes. Then, divide the denominator into the numerator. Carry out the division to four places if needed. You will get a **terminating decimal**, or a **repeating decimal,** which can continue forever. If you get a repeating decimal, then you need to round, usually at two, three, or four places.

a. Terminating decimal: $\frac{1}{5} =$ $\frac{1}{5} = .20$

b. Terminating decimal:

$$\frac{5}{8} = 8\overline{)5.000}$$

.625

$$\begin{array}{r} -48 \\ \hline 20 \\ -16 \\ \hline 40 \\ -40 \\ \hline 0 \end{array}$$

$\frac{5}{8} = .625$

c. Repeating decimal:

.6666

$$\frac{2}{3} = 3\overline{)2.0000}$$

$$\begin{array}{r} -18 \\ \hline 20 \\ -18 \\ \hline 2 \end{array}$$

$\frac{2}{3} = .6666 \ldots .$

May be shortened to .667 or .67

d. Repeating decimal:

.1111

$$\frac{1}{9} = 9\overline{)1.0000}$$

$$\begin{array}{r} -9 \\ \hline 10 \\ -9 \\ \hline 10 \\ -9 \\ \hline 10 \\ -9 \end{array}$$

$\frac{1}{9} = .1111 \ldots .$

May be shortened to .111 or .11
This may also be expressed by writing $.\overline{1}$.
The bar means the decimal repeats.

A Change these fractions to decimals. For repeating decimals, carry out to four places.

1. $\dfrac{1}{2} =$

2. $\dfrac{2}{5} =$

3. $\dfrac{1}{4} =$

4. $\dfrac{1}{8} =$

5. $\dfrac{1}{6} =$

6. $\dfrac{3}{4} =$

7. $\dfrac{1}{3} =$

8. $\dfrac{3}{8} =$

9. $\dfrac{3}{5} =$

10. $\dfrac{5}{12} =$

11. $\dfrac{1}{10} =$

12. $\dfrac{3}{16} =$

13. $\dfrac{1}{20} =$

14. $\dfrac{5}{7} =$

15. $\dfrac{6}{10} =$

16. $\dfrac{2}{9} =$

17. $\dfrac{2}{11} =$

18. $\dfrac{7}{16} =$

19. $\dfrac{2}{15} =$

20. $\dfrac{8}{9} =$

B Change to decimals. For repeating decimals, carry out to four places.

1. $\dfrac{4}{5} =$

2. $\dfrac{1}{12} =$

3. $\dfrac{5}{6} =$

4. $\dfrac{7}{8} =$

5. $\dfrac{2}{19} =$

6. $\dfrac{5}{11} =$

7. $\dfrac{5}{12} =$

8. $\dfrac{7}{10} =$

9. $\dfrac{1}{7} =$

10. $\dfrac{7}{9} =$

11. $\dfrac{2}{10} =$

12. $\dfrac{5}{8} =$

13. $\dfrac{6}{7} =$

14. $\dfrac{9}{11} =$

15. $\dfrac{1}{16} =$

16. $\dfrac{7}{15} =$

17. $\dfrac{5}{12} =$

18. $\dfrac{2}{13} =$

19. $\dfrac{3}{22} =$

20. $\dfrac{4}{25} =$

Changing Decimals to Percents

To change a decimal to a percent, first move the decimal point **two places to the right**. Then substitute the percent sign (%) for the decimal point. A percent can be greater than 100%, such as 105%, 275%, or 550%. As decimals, these percents are written 1.0, 1.05, 2.75, and 5.5. Thus, when you see a whole number to the left of a decimal, you still move the decimal point two places to the right and substitute the percent sign.

Examples:

a.   .82 = 82%   d.   1.8 = 180%

b.   .1 = 10%   e.   .125 = 12.5%

c.   .35 = 35%

The answer in example *e,* 12.5%, can be expressed as a fraction too: $12\frac{1}{2}$%. The decimal portion, (.5, or $\frac{5}{10}$), is changed to $\frac{1}{2}$ by reducing: $\frac{5}{10} = \frac{1}{2}$.

Write these decimals as percents.

1. .5 =	.63 =	.48 =	.99 =
2. .80 =	.05 =	.4 =	.2 =
3. 1.10 =	.40 =	1.01 =	.60 =
4. .9 =	2.03 =	.75 =	.55 =
5. 3.08 =	4.25 =	.04 =	1.7 =
6. .7 =	.12 =	.68 =	.175 =
7. .1875 =	.625 =	.4375 =	.3333 =

Changing Percents to Decimals

To change a percent to a decimal, first drop the percent sign (%). Then, move the decimal point two places to the left and insert a decimal point. Use zero as a place holder if the percent is a one–place number. (Any number from 0 to 9 is a one-place number.) If a fraction is part of the percent, it must be changed to decimal form the same way you would change a fraction to a decimal. (examples: $\frac{1}{2}$ = .5, $\frac{1}{3}$ = .33, and so forth)

Examples:

a.   30% = .30

b.   65% = .65

c.   2% = .02

d. $8\frac{3}{4}$%

> First change $\frac{3}{4}$ to percent form. $4\overline{)3.00}$ → $.75$

> Rewrite the percent: 8.75%

> Next, drop the percent sign and move the decimal point **two places** to the left: .0875

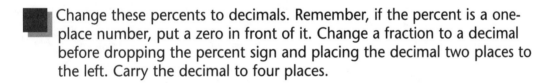

Change these percents to decimals. Remember, if the percent is a one-place number, put a zero in front of it. Change a fraction to a decimal before dropping the percent sign and placing the decimal two places to the left. Carry the decimal to four places.

1.   25% =   3% =   72% =   82% =

2.   8% =   75% =   11% =   63% =

3. $1\frac{1}{2}$% = $4\frac{1}{5}$% = $7\frac{2}{3}$% = $16\frac{1}{6}$% =

4. $3\frac{1}{3}$% = $18\frac{3}{4}$% = $6\frac{5}{6}$% = $40\frac{2}{3}$% =

**U
N
I
T**

3

Many items are purchased by amounts such as dozens (doz.), pounds (lb.), and yards (yd.), and the cost is usually stated as such. However, when you don't want the whole amount, the part you want is called the **fractional quantity.** The cost is found by multiplying the price by the fractional quantity.

Example: Fresh peanuts are priced at $1.99 a pound. You wish to purchase $\frac{1}{4}$ of a pound. The cost would be found as follows:

First, write the example the way you write a whole number and a fraction when mulitplying. Use the number 1 as the denominator for the money amount.

$$\frac{\$1.99}{1} \times \frac{1}{4}$$

Second, multiply the top and bottom rows straight across. If the answer is an improper fraction, it cannot stay that way. We must divide as we would ordinary numbers.

$$\frac{\$1.99}{1} \times \frac{1}{4} = \frac{\$1.99}{4} = 4\overline{)1.99}$$

$$\begin{array}{r} .49 \\ 4\overline{)1.99} \\ -\underline{16} \\ 39 \\ -\underline{36} \\ 3 \end{array}$$

Since money is involved, there can be no remainder, because a penny cannot be divided into parts.

If the money does not come out even, add a penny (.01) to your answer. Money is always rounded up.

This process is called rounding money. This is what was done in the example— the answer is $.50. Therefore, $\frac{1}{4}$ pound of peanuts at $1.99 a pound would cost you $.50.

Study examples *a* through *h*. Can you tell why the money was rounded or why it was not rounded?

a.
$$\begin{array}{r} \$0.79 \\ 5\overline{)\$3.95} \\ \underline{-\ 0} \\ 39 \\ \underline{-\ 35} \\ 45 \\ \underline{-\ 45} \\ 00 \end{array}$$
= $.79

e.
$$\begin{array}{r} \$0.59 \\ 7\overline{)\$4.18} \\ \underline{-\ 0} \\ 41 \\ \underline{-\ 35} \\ 68 \\ \underline{-\ 63} \\ 5 \end{array}$$
= $.60

b.
$$\begin{array}{r} \$0.35 \\ 9\overline{)\$3.16} \\ \underline{-\ 0} \\ 31 \\ \underline{-\ 27} \\ 46 \\ \underline{-\ 45} \\ 1 \end{array}$$
= $.36

f.
= $9.28

c.
$$\begin{array}{r} \$.07 \\ 4\overline{)\$.30} \\ \underline{-\ 0} \\ 30 \\ \underline{-\ 28} \\ 20 \end{array}$$
= $.08

g.
$$\begin{array}{r} \$.05 \\ 12\overline{)\$.63} \\ \underline{-\ 0} \\ 63 \\ \underline{-\ 60} \\ 3 \end{array}$$
= $.06

d.
$$\begin{array}{r} \$.66 \\ 3\overline{)\$1.99} \\ \underline{-\ 18} \\ 19 \\ \underline{-\ 18} \\ 1 \end{array}$$
= $.67

h.
$$\begin{array}{r} \$.83 \\ 6\overline{)\$4.98} \\ \underline{-\ 48} \\ 18 \\ \underline{-\ 18} \\ 0 \end{array}$$
= $.83

Study the examples.

$$6)\overline{\$60.94} \begin{array}{l} \$10.15 \\ \hline \end{array} = \$10.16$$

$$\begin{array}{r} \$10.15 \\ 6)\overline{\$60.94} \\ \underline{-\ 6} \\ 00 \\ \underline{-\ 00} \\ 9 \\ \underline{-\ 6} \\ 34 \\ \underline{-\ 30} \\ 4 \end{array}$$

A Divide and round to the next cent if necessary.

1. $8)\overline{\$6.40}$

2. $7)\overline{\$3.58}$

3. $17)\overline{\$3.48}$

4. $4)\overline{\$3.32}$

5. $4)\overline{\$.23}$

6. $8)\overline{\$.72}$

7. $12)\overline{\$4.67}$

8. $2)\overline{\$3.95}$

B Divide and round to the next cent if necessary.

1. 6)$24.12

2. 5)$10.99

3. 3)$7.31

4. 8)$.55

5. 12)$17.94

6. 4)$82.45

7. 9)$60.00

8. 3)$19.95

9. 2)$.33

10. 25)$5.75

11. 7)$17.88

12. 21)$8.48

13. 32)$29.64

14. 18)$34.34

15. 4)$23.00

C Divide and round to the next cent if necessary.

1. 3)$5.55

2. 12)$1,149.50

3. 5)$7.98

4. 6)$7.77

5. 24)$14.88

6. 3)$9.57

7. 4)$6.60

8. 36)$479.77

9. 6)$6.99

10. 2)$2.99

11. 9)$1,008.00

12. 7)$5.88

13. 8)$3.49

14. 12)$359.50

15. 4)$5.00

16. 7)$6.99

17. 24)$32.32

18. 2)$7.50

Fractions and Prices

Study these examples.

a. If oranges are priced at $2.53 a doz., how much would $\frac{2}{3}$ of a doz. cost?

$$\frac{\$2.53}{1} \times \frac{2}{3} = \frac{\$5.06}{3} = 3\overline{)\begin{array}{l} \$1.68 = \$1.69 \\ \$5.06 \end{array}}$$

$$\begin{array}{r} -\ 3 \\ \hline 20 \\ -\ 18 \\ \hline 26 \\ -\ 24 \\ \hline 2 \end{array}$$

b. Carpet runner sells for $13.69 a yd. How much would you charge for $1\frac{5}{8}$ yd.?

$$\frac{\$13.69}{1} \times \frac{13}{8} = \frac{\$177.97}{8} = 8\overline{)\begin{array}{l} \$22.24 = \$22.25 \\ \$177.97 \end{array}}$$

$$\begin{array}{r} -\ 16 \\ \hline 17 \\ -\ 16 \\ \hline 19 \\ -\ 16 \\ \hline 37 \\ -\ 32 \\ \hline 5 \end{array}$$

c. If steak sells for $4.69 a pound, how much will you charge for a steak weighing $\frac{7}{8}$ lb.?

$$\frac{\$4.69}{1} \times \frac{7}{8} = \frac{\$32.83}{8} = 8\overline{)\begin{array}{l} \$4.10 = \$4.11 \\ \$32.83 \end{array}}$$

$$\begin{array}{r} -\ 32 \\ \hline 8 \\ -\ 8 \\ \hline 3 \end{array}$$

UNIT 3

A Find how much you would charge for each purchase below.

1. $\frac{1}{2}$ dozen eggs at $1.39 a doz.

2. $\frac{2}{3}$ yards of copper wiring at $2.87 a yd.

3. $\frac{1}{4}$ pound of butter at $2.25 a lb.

4. $2\frac{1}{2}$ dozen potted plants at $3.29 doz.

5. $3\frac{1}{2}$ yards of self–stick vinyl at $2.49 a yd.

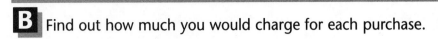

B Find out how much you would charge for each purchase.

1. $\frac{5}{6}$ of a dozen oranges at $2.54 a doz.

2. $\frac{5}{8}$ of a yard of corduroy at $6.95 a yd.

3. $\frac{1}{2}$ dozen lemons at $2.39 a doz.

4. $\frac{1}{2}$ pound of cashew nuts at $4.77 a lb.

5. $\frac{1}{3}$ pound of veal at $8.97 a lb.

6. $\frac{1}{2}$ gallon of paint at $14.99 a gal.

C Find the cost of each purchase.

1. $\frac{5}{6}$ of a ton of gravel at $97.50 a ton

2. $\frac{5}{8}$ gallon of a tile glue at $12.99 a gallon

3. $4\frac{3}{4}$ yards of carpet runner at $15.69 a yard

4. $\frac{7}{8}$ yards of tie silk at $35.77 a yard

5. $\frac{1}{2}$ gallon of olive oil at $22.97 a gallon

6. $\frac{2}{3}$ yards of plastic tubing at $1.89 a yard

7. $\frac{1}{2}$ bushel of apples at $18.99 a bushel

8. $\frac{2}{3}$ of a ream of paper at $43.50 a ream

9. $\frac{5}{8}$ kilo of dried fruit at $8.79 a kilo

10. $\frac{3}{4}$ of a liter of kerosene at $1.74 a liter

D Find the cost of each purchase below. Remember: put dollar signs and decimal points in the right places.

1. $\frac{3}{4}$ tons of sand at $49.85 a ton

2. $\frac{1}{3}$ ounce of dill weed at $1.99 per oz.

3. $\frac{2}{3}$ dozen grapefruit at $5.39 a doz.

4. $\frac{7}{9}$ yard of ribbon at $2.37 a yd.

5. $1\frac{3}{4}$ gallons of gasoline at $1.39 a gal.

6. $\frac{3}{4}$ dozen goldfish at $12.98 per doz.

7. $\frac{2}{3}$ pound of lawn seed at $4.59 per lb.

8. $\frac{1}{8}$ of a pound of cheese at $4.84 per lb.

9. $\frac{1}{4}$ kilo of peaches at $4.56 per kilo

10. $\frac{1}{2}$ pound of lunch meat at $2.93 per lb.

UNIT 4

Counting Change

Lesson 1

When you buy an item at a store, you usually receive change. Just to make sure you received the correct amount, you should count it.

A cashier or clerk in a store also should be careful to give a customer the correct change and count it the right way.

Change is usually given in the **fewest number of coins.** The person giving change should repeat the **price** of the item and then count, starting with the smallest coins.

Example: A customer gives you $1.00 to pay for a $.34 purchase. How would you count the change?

Solution: First repeat the price of the purchase. Then give the customer a penny and say $.34, and $.01 is $.35, and $.05 is $.40, and $.10 is $.50, and $.25 is $.75, and $.25 is $1.00.

The following exercises will give you practice in counting change. The numbers in Column A give the amount of the purchase and the fewest number of coins needed to make $1.00. Column B gives the amount of the purchase. Count the coins as you would if you were giving change to a customer.

Examples:

a.

A	B
$.85	$.85
.05	.90
.10	1.00

b.

A	B
$.33	$.33
.01	.34
.01	.35
.05	.40
.10	.50
.25	.75
.25	1.00

c.

A	B
$.16	$.16
.01	.17
.01	.18
.01	.19
.01	.20
.05	.25
.25	.50
.25	.75
.25	1.00

d.

A	B
$.57	$.57
.01	.58
.01	.59
.01	.60
.05	.65
.10	.75
.25	1.00

A Practice counting the change to $1.00.

	A	B			A	B			A	B
1.	$.14	$.14	**2.**	$.45	$.45	**3.**	$.07	$.07
	.01			.05			.01	
	.10			.25			.01	
	.25			.25			.01	
	.25						.05	
	.25						.10	
							.25	
							.25	
							.25	

	A	B			A	B			A	B
4.	$.77	$.77	**5.**	$.28	$.28	**6.**	$.49	$.49
	.01			.01			.01	
	.01			.01			.25	
	.01			.10			.25	
	.10			.10				
	.10			.50				

	A	B			A	B			A	B
7.	$.32	$.32	**8.**	$.63	$.63	**9.**	$.71	$.71
	.01			.01			.01	
	.01			.01			.01	
	.01			.10			.01	
	.05			.25			.01	
	.10						.25	
	.25							
	.25							

	A	B			A	B			A	B
10.	$.45	$.45	**11.**	$.22	$.22	**12.**	$.15	$.15
	.05			.01			.10	
	.25			.01			.25	
	.25			.01			.50	
				.25				
				.25				
				.25				

B Practice counting change to $1.00.

1.	A	B
	$.18	$.18
	.01	
	.01	
	.05	
	.25	
	.50	

2.	A	B
	$.27	$.27
	.01	
	.01	
	.01	
	.10	
	.10	
	.25	
	.25	

3.	A	B
	$.66	$.66
	.01	
	.01	
	.01	
	.01	
	.05	
	.25	

4.	A	B
	$.29	$.29
	.01	
	.10	
	.10	
	.25	
	.25	

5.	A	B
	$.46	$.46
	.01	
	.01	
	.01	
	.01	
	.50	

6.	A	B
	$.20	$.20
	.05	
	.25	
	.50	

7.	A	B
	$.25	$.25
	.25	
	.25	
	.25	

8.	A	B
	$.42	$.42
	.01	
	.01	
	.01	
	.05	
	.25	
	.25	

9.	A	B
	$.15	$.15
	.10	
	.25	
	.25	
	.25	

10.	A	B
	$.55	$.55
	.10	
	.10	
	.25	

11.	A	B
	$.23	$.23
	.01	
	.01	
	.25	
	.50	

12.	A	B
	$.79	$.79
	.01	
	.10	
	.10	

Counting Coins

A On the chart, figure out the correct change to give to a customer. Use the fewest coins. Rows *a* and *b* are examples.

	Price	Amount Given	$.01 Pennies	$.05 Nickels	$.10 Dimes	$.25 Quarters	$.50 Half Dollars	Amount of Change
a.	$.67	$1.00	3	1		1		$.33
b.	.41	1.00	4	1			1	.59
1.	.25	1.00						
2.	.37	1.00						
3.	.46	1.00						
4.	.68	1.00						
5.	.19	1.00						
6.	.33	1.00						
7.	.29	.50						
8.	.78	1.00						
9.	.36	1.00						
10.	.27	1.00						
11.	.14	1.00						
12.	.60	1.00						
13.	.26	1.00						
14.	.08	1.00						
15.	.43	1.00						
16.	.88	1.00						
17.	.75	1.00						
18.	.11	.50						
19.	.39	1.00						
20.	.16	.50						

UNIT 4

B On the chart, figure out the correct change to give to a customer. Use the fewest coins. Rows *a* and *b* are examples.

	Price	Amount Given	$.01 Pennies	$.05 Nickels	$.10 Dimes	$.25 Quarters	$.50 Half Dollars	Amount of Change
a.	$.16	$1.00	4	1		3		$.84
b.	.43	.50	2	1				.07
1.	.07	.50						
2.	.47	1.00						
3.	.53	1.00						
4.	.16	.25						
5.	.21	.25						
6.	.74	.75						
7.	.69	.75						
8.	.81	.85						
9.	.37	.50						
10.	.52	.75						
11.	.19	.50						
12.	.22	1.00						
13.	.75	.80						
14.	.21	.50						
15.	.13	.20						
16.	.86	1.00						
17.	.17	.25						
18.	.49	.60						
19.	.31	.50						
20.	.55	.75						

End-of Book Test

A Add.

1. $1\frac{1}{3}$
$\quad 1\frac{1}{2}$
$+ 3\frac{1}{6}$

2. $5\frac{4}{5}$
$\quad 2\frac{1}{4}$
$+ 7\frac{9}{10}$

3. $2\frac{2}{3}$
$\quad 3\frac{3}{4}$
$+ 5\frac{5}{6}$

4. $2\frac{1}{8}$
$\quad 1\frac{3}{4}$
$+ 1\frac{2}{3}$

5. $2\frac{1}{9}$
$\quad 1\frac{1}{3}$
$+ 4\frac{1}{2}$

6. $5\frac{1}{4}$
$\quad 2\frac{1}{12}$
$+ 3\frac{1}{6}$

7. $5\frac{1}{10}$
$\quad 2\frac{1}{2}$
$+ 1\frac{3}{5}$

8. $2\frac{1}{9}$
$\quad 3\frac{1}{2}$
$\quad 6\frac{2}{3}$

9. $3\frac{5}{8}$
$\quad 4\frac{3}{4}$
$\quad 3\frac{1}{2}$

B Subtract.

1. $\quad \frac{1}{2}$
$- \frac{3}{10}$

2. $3\frac{2}{3}$
$- 2\frac{1}{5}$

3. $54\frac{1}{2}$
$- 19\frac{3}{5}$

4. $9\frac{1}{8}$
$- 1\frac{3}{16}$

5. $10\frac{3}{4}$
$- 6\frac{7}{10}$

6. $9\frac{5}{6}$
$- 7\frac{7}{8}$

7. $\quad \frac{3}{5}$
$- \frac{2}{7}$

8. $16\frac{5}{8}$
$- 1\frac{3}{4}$

9. $20\frac{1}{5}$
$- 10\frac{1}{4}$

C Multiply.

1. $4 \times 2\frac{1}{2} =$

2. $15 \times 1\frac{2}{3} =$

3. $\frac{7}{8} \times 1\frac{3}{4} =$

4. $7\frac{1}{2} \times 3\frac{2}{3} =$

5. $3\frac{2}{3} \times 9 =$

6. $2\frac{3}{5} \times 1\frac{1}{6} =$

7. $3 \times 5\frac{1}{3} =$

8. $4\frac{1}{4} \times \frac{1}{7} =$

9. $2\frac{1}{5} \times 9 =$

10. $7 \times \frac{1}{2} =$

11. $9\frac{1}{6} \times 1\frac{3}{5} =$

12. $6\frac{2}{3} \times 1\frac{1}{8} =$

D Divide.

1. $\frac{3}{5} \div 3 =$

2. $6 \div \frac{3}{8} =$

3. $\frac{5}{8} \div \frac{3}{4} =$

4. $4 \div \frac{2}{3} =$

5. $6\frac{1}{5} \div \frac{1}{5} =$

6. $2\frac{1}{2} \div 4\frac{1}{4} =$

7. $2\frac{3}{4} \div 3 =$

8. $6\frac{1}{4} \div 2\frac{1}{2} =$

9. $3 \div \frac{3}{4} =$

10. $\frac{5}{12} \div 2\frac{1}{6} =$

11. $3\frac{1}{8} \div 1\frac{3}{4} =$

12. $2\frac{1}{6} \div 1\frac{2}{3} =$

E Write these percents as decimals.

1. 4% =
2. 25% =
3. 18% =
4. 3% =
5. $2\frac{1}{5}$% =
6. 40% =
7. 35% =
8. $3\frac{1}{4}$% =
9. $33\frac{1}{3}$% =
10. 50% =
11. 7.5% =
12. 8.75% =
13. 3.5% =
14. $7\frac{3}{4}$% =
15. 8.125% =

16. 9.625% =
17. 11.75% =
18. $6\frac{1}{2}$% =
19. $60\frac{1}{2}$% =
20. 11.66% =
21. 33.3% =
22. 5.16% =
23. 13.375% =
24. 18.5% =
25. $17\frac{1}{2}$% =
26. 9.1818% =
27. 3.16% =
28. 105% =
29. 260% =
30. 114% =

F Change these mixed numbers to improper fractions.

1. $1\frac{1}{3}$ =
2. $3\frac{1}{2}$ =
3. $1\frac{3}{4}$ =
4. $4\frac{3}{8}$ =
5. $2\frac{1}{5}$ =
6. $8\frac{2}{5}$ =
7. $1\frac{3}{7}$ =

8. $10\frac{2}{3}$ =
9. $4\frac{5}{7}$ =
10. $6\frac{4}{5}$ =
11. $3\frac{7}{8}$ =
12. $5\frac{1}{6}$ =
13. $6\frac{1}{2}$ =
14. $1\frac{3}{16}$ =

15. $9\frac{3}{5}$ =
16. $6\frac{2}{5}$ =
17. $7\frac{3}{10}$ =
18. $3\frac{4}{9}$ =
19. $2\frac{1}{4}$ =
20. $2\frac{1}{3}$ =
21. $3\frac{3}{4}$ =

22. $6\frac{4}{5}$ =
23. $3\frac{5}{6}$ =
24. $10\frac{1}{4}$ =
25. $9\frac{1}{3}$ =
26. $9\frac{3}{7}$ =
27. $4\frac{1}{4}$ =
28. $7\frac{1}{9}$ =

G Divide and round off to the next cent.

1. $2\overline{)\$.56}$ 2. $13\overline{)\$3.69}$ 3. $12\overline{)\$17.88}$ 4. $12\overline{)\$13.49}$

5. $7\overline{)\$.50}$ 6. $6\overline{)\$7.77}$ 7. $25\overline{)\$4.99}$ 8. $60\overline{)\$17.75}$

9. $2\overline{)\$5.79}$ 10. $9\overline{)\$19.95}$ 11. $3\overline{)\$7.62}$ 12. $6\overline{)\$7.97}$

13. $8\overline{)\$5.64}$ 14. $144\overline{)\$20}$ 15. $5\overline{)\$.49}$ 16. $12\overline{)\$28.28}$

H Change these improper fractions to a whole number or a mixed number.

1. $\dfrac{30}{6} =$ 2. $5\dfrac{5}{10} =$ 3. $\dfrac{132}{11} =$

4. $\dfrac{27}{4} =$ 5. $\dfrac{39}{13} =$ 6. $\dfrac{97}{8} =$

7. $\dfrac{14}{8} =$ 8. $\dfrac{10}{3} =$ 9. $\dfrac{105}{15} =$

10. $\dfrac{9}{5} =$ 11. $\dfrac{16}{5} =$ 12. $\dfrac{54}{11} =$

13. $\dfrac{13}{3} =$ 14. $\dfrac{56}{14} =$ 15. $\dfrac{5}{3} =$

16. $\dfrac{21}{10} =$ 17. $\dfrac{44}{11} =$ 18. $\dfrac{17}{2} =$

19. $\dfrac{15}{2} =$ 20. $\dfrac{17}{3} =$ 21. $\dfrac{17}{6} =$

22. $\dfrac{22}{7} =$ 23. $\dfrac{19}{9} =$ 24. $\dfrac{19}{12} =$

I Read each problem carefully. Then solve it in the space provided.

1. Sue had $14\frac{1}{6}$ yards of speaker wire to connect stereo speakers. She used $13\frac{1}{3}$ yards. How much did she have left?

_____

2. Max bought a sweater for $45.98, a pair of jeans for $36.00, and a pair of shoes for $47.50. He gave the clerk $150. How much change should he get?

_____

3. Soledad bought $\frac{1}{2}$ pound of cheese at $6.79 a pound. How much change should she get from a $5 bill?

_____

4. If eggs are marked 2 dozen for $2.97, how much will 4 dozen cost?

_____

5. If eggs are marked 2 dozen for $2.97, how much will 1 dozen cost?

_____

6. Mai Lin is learning to play the piano. The first day she practiced $\frac{1}{2}$ hour in the morning, $\frac{3}{4}$ hour in the afternoon, and $\frac{3}{4}$ hour in the early evening. How many hours did she practice?

_____

7. Hector has to paint 1,510 square feet. One gallon of paint will cover 400 square feet. He can get 3 gallons of paint for $29.88. How much will it cost to complete the job?

_____

8. Safeena needs to plan a menu for her club's lunch. Twelve will attend, but two are guests and will not be contributing. The others will each contribute $10. How much can she spend per serving?

_____

9. Orrin takes private half-hour guitar lessons at $17.50 per half hour. He'd like to take as many lessons as possible and can budget $60 monthly. How many lessons can he take? _____

10. Arkadia needs to make 150 copies of her résumé and can get them for $.07$\frac{1}{2}$ each. How much will 150 cost? _____

11. Boris can repair bicycle inner tubes in about ten minutes. If he gets $1.75 per repair, how much can he average earning hourly? _____

12. Winona's dog-walking service earns her $4.50 for each half-hour walk. She also needs about ten minutes to get from job to job. How much can she earn in five hours? _____

J Count the correct change in each example below. Use the fewest number of coins.

			Coins Given in Change					
	Price	Amount Given	$.01 Pennies	$.05 Nickels	$.10 Dimes	$.25 Quarters	$.50 Half Dollars	Amount of Change
1.	.03	1.00						
2.	.67	1.00						
3.	.15	1.00						
4.	.98	1.00						
5.	.07	1.00						
6.	.43	.50						
7.	.77	1.00						
8.	.19	.50						
9.	.18	1.00						
10.	.63	.75						